THE POWER OF THE LOVING MAN

LIZ LEWINSON

Other books by Liz Lewinson

American Buddhist Rebel:
The Story of Rama - Dr. Frederick Lenz

Independence Ring

Women, Meditation and Power

THE POWER OF THE LOVING MAN

LIZ LEWINSON

SKYE
PEARL

Copyright © 2020 by Liz Lewinson
The Power of the Loving Man

Published 2020 by Skye Pearl
Sausalito, CA USA

ISBN: 978-0-9898899-6-4 (Paperback)
ISBN: 978-0-9898899-7-1 (eBook)

Publisher's Cataloging-In-Publication Data
(Prepared by The Donohue Group, Inc.)

Names: Lewinson, Liz, author.
Title: The power of the loving man / Liz Lewinson.
Description: Sausalito, CA USA : Skye Pearl, 2020. |
Includes bibliographical references.
Identifiers: ISBN 9780989889964 (paperback) | ISBN 9780989889971 (ebook)
Subjects: LCSH: Men--Psychology. | Sex role--Psychological aspects. | Masculinity. | Love.
Classification: LCC BF692.5 .L49 2020 (print) | LCC BF692.5 (ebook) | DDC 155.332--dc23

ALL RIGHTS RESERVED

The scanning, uploading and distribution of this book via the Internet or via any other means without the permission of the publisher is illegal and punishable by law. Please purchase only authorized electronic editions, and do not participate in or encourage electronic piracy of copyrighted materials. Your support of the author's rights is appreciated.

The Author and the Publisher accept no responsibility for inaccuracies or omissions, and speci ically disclaim any liability, loss, or risk, whether personal, inancial, or otherwise, that is incurred as a consequence, directly or indirectly, from the use and/or application of any of the contents of this book.

Cover art by Brains & Riots Creative Studio

This book is dedicated to boys and men
and their innate loving kindness.

"There's a lot of us out here that are birds, man. We all need to just fly."

— Travis Scott

TABLE OF CONTENTS

Introduction ix
1. The Teaching. 1
2. Pondering Power. 7
3. The Vision. 17
4. Power Shift 25
5. The Challenge for Men. 35
6. What's Love Got to Do with It?. 41
7. Vast (Big!) Love. 49
8. Man-Obstacles. 55
9. The Diamond Ecosystem of Love. 69
10. Meditate! 89
11. Sex 101
12. Polishing the Diamond. 109

13. Negotiate the Street 117

14. Relationships and Role-Playing. 123

15. More Meditation 137

16. If You Want Love.................... 141

17. Avoiding the Anger Patch............. 143

18. Dancing for Men..................... 149

19. We Are Both Male and Female......... 163

20. The Power of the Loving Man......... 169

Appendix: How to Get a Date 171

Liz Lewinson 175

INTRODUCTION

The power of love snuck up on me, hugged the center of my chest, and caused me to write this book.

For several years, giving talks on *Women, Meditation, and Power* at bookstores, libraries, classrooms, private homes, yoga studios, auditoriums, and meditation halls, I spoke about the vast, innate power of women and the loving kindness innate in men. I focused on the power of women, which has been misunderstood and underestimated for so long.

Then I realized something was missing.

I could not just focus on the power of women to primarily female audiences because as I looked around and saw women becoming more powerful, I did not see a similar happy transition in men.

Instead, I saw men become increasingly frustrated and uncomfortable with the rising power of women. I saw some men becoming more hostile and violent in their rejection of the pervasive and positive social change. I sensed some men feeling fear.

I increasingly saw men unwilling or unable to relinquish their old thought patterns about manness and womanness, even if some of those patterns were acquired in the fourth grade. In many cases, I saw men—some at the leading edge of tech and innovation—still mired in a limited view of what it means to be a man. THIS is what a man is, with "this" a narrowly defined box.

I sensed a yearning within men not to be misunderstood or belittled but to find their own best voice. Something that they would be proud of, that they could grow and truly live with.

Most men are not resistant to change. They wonder what and how to change.

My heart felt compassion, not condescension. Even if men have repressed women for millennia, which they have, as the old saying goes, two wrongs do not make a right. It would be wrong to withhold insight and liberation for men.

I felt compelled to find out, to conduct interviews, to know what happened to men to give them a false view of women and of themselves. I wanted to learn what makes men unaware of their own highest quality—love. By "love," I do not mean romantic love but a love far deeper, more inclusive, encompassing all of the earth and humanity. A pure, profound love that resides securely in one's being and is not tossed aside by circumstance.

In many languages, there are two or more words for love. One word is set aside for romantic love. The other terms cover a more overarching love, such as deep affection, appreciation, or selflessness. Languages that offer more than one word for love include Japanese, Hungarian, Spanish, Tamil, Sanskrit, Pali, and Greek.

Ancient Greece employed anywhere between three and ten terms for love, depending on who was telling the story. (Come to think of it, "ancient" Greece was only about 3,000 years ago, a mere blink of the eye in cosmological time. So rather than debunking these terms as "ancient," I think it's fair to consider their likelihood today.)

- *Eros*: sexual passion and desire, tends to burn out quickly
- *Ludus*: playfulness in love, childlike innocence
- *Pragma*: longstanding, enduring love; a unique harmony that forms over time

- *Philia*: friendship, loyalty, camaraderie without physical attraction
- *Philautia*: self-love that is not narcissism but is based on acceptance and self-compassion
- *Storge*: love for family and longstanding, familiar communities
- *Agape*: selfless, unconditional love, boundless compassion and empathy, universal loving kindness

In the Buddhist Pali language, *metta* is a term frequently used to describe goodwill, loving kindness, universal love, a feeling of friendliness and heartfelt concern for all living beings, human or non-human, in all situations. The chief mark of metta is a benevolent attitude: a keen desire to promote the welfare of others. It is said that "metta subdues the vice of hatred in all its varied shades: anger, ill will, aversion, and resentment."[1]

These wide-ranging definitions of love still work. This book will touch on all forms of love including *eros*. At the end of the day, developing all

---

[1] Bogoda, Robert, "A Simple Guide to Life,: 1994, https://www.wisdomlib.org/buddhism/essay/a-simple-guide-to-life/d/doc2149.html

forms of love will give you a much more fulfilling experience of *eros*.

You cannot truly experience any of the types of love—let alone *agape*, unconditional love—if you have a false view of males and females, of yourself and others.

From my own experience, I know that love of great depth and humility comes from stillness. When you are still inside, you can truly love.

While I identify as a female, I can write about the loving nature of men because I know stillness. I have been practicing making my mind still (this is what meditation is) for over 50 years. I am an authority on stillness from which love emanates.

Love is gender free, but there are qualities of male and female energy bodies that differ, making it more powerful and intense for one gender than another to express and manifest love.

Men and women have both love and power in their beings. In deep stillness, no thought in the mind, in light, these qualities merge and emerge.

As a writer, teacher, compassionate being, and meditator, I made a decision. Now is the time to collect what I know and to share what I have seen and learned so that men and women of every sexual or asexual orientation or gender identity may experience stillness and perspective and revel in their highest qualities.

Yes, misogyny (hatred, dislike, or mistrust of women) is deep rooted and embedded in society. This matters because unless women are free to be who they are, men cannot be truly and happily themselves.

Based on my conversations with many people, I know men are still caught in a rigid maze of false ideas about women and themselves.

These writings explore the sources of this dilemma and the path out.

1
THE TEACHING

The beginning of my life of insight into the power of women and the loving kindness of men began in the early 80s. No one was talking about female power and new forms of masculinity then. In fact, looking back, every form of male superiority (and female acceptance of that role) oozed through work environments, entertainment, media, families, politics and more.

So when I heard teachings years ago from a respected Buddhist teacher on the topic of men and women, it was shocking and life changing. It was this teacher who exposed the root of the problem. He rang the bell for my wakeup call, and the reverberations have radiated in my head ever since.

The talk was about women and enlightenment. A friend wanted me to attend. I went because…I was a friend.

The teacher was young and funny. The talk was held at the Beverly Theatre in Beverly Hills, and the hall was full. I get impatient during talks, but this one, delivered without props, slides, or blackboard, grabbed my attention.

Soon, I was writing down every word on a purse-size notepad.

Men, he said, are energetically structured to support love and humility. Women are wired for power.

Men and women have bodies of energy that surround their physical bodies. Energy centers in the body are often referred to in yoga or tai chi classes and may be termed the "subtle physical body." In martial arts, discussions of the *ki* or *chi* relate to energy surrounding the physical body. All bodies and objects emanate some form energy.

A woman's energy body conducts life force much more rapidly than a man's energy body, the teacher explained. Her body of energy is very fluid and vibrates rapidly, resembling a butterfly's wings that extend outward, way beyond her physical body. Her energy body is less dense than a man's, which means her circuitry is also more sensitive to negative emotions and feelings. Her energy body emanates power.

A man's energy body is denser, more grid-shaped, and held like a multifaceted network of lines closer to the physical body. It conducts energy or life force more slowly, but it can withstand negative emotions and feelings more easily than a woman's energy body. The less rapid energetic circuitry in a man's energy body makes him a perfect vehicle for all manifestations of love and kindness.

The rapid vibration or life force of a woman's energy body makes a woman by nature literally more powerful than a man.

It is human nature to try to destroy what one is threatened by.

In our times (the last 10,000 years or so), men, threatened by the power of women, tried to destroy that power in every way – religiously, economically, philosophically, socially, sexually, physically. The suppression of all aspects of a woman's innate life force has been going on for so long that women themselves have forgotten about the vast natural power of their inner being.

Countless generations of men have grown up feeling superior to women, a deep-rooted sentiment that is not true. No one is superior to anyone else. A feeling of superiority creates bad karma for the person who harbors this sentiment. This situation is bad for men, and even worse for women. And disastrous for the planet.

If a man feels superior to a woman and overtly or subtly tries to suppress her power, he is in a lower state of mind. The teacher explained that karma is not just if you hit someone, they or someone else will hit you back. Karma is your state of mind.

If a woman, in order to survive oppression, uses her fluid life force to blast a man with the power of her sexual energy to attract him, she is in the mind-set of manipulation. That is a low state of mind for her – bad karma.

From my notes –

For men, the karmic retribution for the oppression of women is to find themselves enwrapped in emotions and feelings that are not indigenous to them (i.e., superiority, false sexuality, domination, fear of expressing emotions, and the need to control).

Instead of directing their attention toward the many forms of loving kindness, which is natural for men, they direct their attention toward a limited experience of domination of people and events. They focus on sexuality, feeling that they are highly sexual when they're not. This causes anger and turmoil in men.

Males and females are equally powerful. But power and other qualities manifest differently through males and females. There's no need to feel superior or inferior. All there is, is the need to be.

You have to become both a man and a woman. You must accept what is real and what is true. To do that, you must examine yourself, your history, and simply start to observe.

Observe. Watch or feel how women use their life force to make men feel more sexual. And watch how men, through their ideas that repress female power, project a field of attention that limits and holds back women.

Here is a prescient quote from the talk I attended several decades ago:

"The most important problem for our world to solve is the inequality of men and women. When women come into their full power, a balance will occur which has not been seen for so long that no one remembers it. The greatest pain is suffered by women. And as long as men keep women out of balance and hold them back, they hold themselves back. That's their karma. I think the greatest need in this world is the liberation of women and when that occurs, all will be liberated. There will be a new world. If that does not occur, then I think you will see the dissolution of the world we live in."[2]

When I heard these teachings, I was blown away. It was the '80s, and I had been raised to seek and marry a man more powerful than myself. When I found out that I would never find one, that I was the power being, I felt like a balloon in the sky.

I was free to be who I actually was. Men were free to be who they are.

---

[2] Lenz, Frederick, "Why Don't More Women Attain Enlightenment," Insights: Talks on the Nature of Existence, 1983.

2

PONDERING POWER

When I left the theater that night, and for many years afterward, I pondered power. I was confused about what the term meant. The idea of power made me nervous.

When searching for "power" in the dictionary, I discovered that misleading terms abound. Words like physical might, control, authority, or influence over others seemed limiting and superficial.

I decided my role model should be power in nature, the most striking, enduring, and visible manifestation of power. Even a nuclear bomb does not come close to the power of a Category 5 hurricane, which is estimated to be similar to 10,000 nuclear bombs.[3] Humans are reminded of

---

[3] Biello, David, "Hurricane Force," Scientific American, 2006, https://www.scientificamerican.com/article/hurricane-force/

their utter powerlessness when nature shows her ultimate strength, so I decided to make Mother Nature my worthy example of the real nature of power.

First, I looked at power sources. We know so much more now about the generation of power than we used to. Think about hydroelectric power and how it is generated. Electricity is created through fluidity and change. Electrical generation is the transformation of motion energy into electrical energy. Most of US electricity generation is from electric power plants that use turbines or similar machines to drive electricity generators. Cascading water in dams rushes through chutes and drives turbines.

Tidal power is produced through the use of tidal energy generators. Large underwater turbines are placed in areas with high tidal movements and are designed to capture the kinetic motion of the ebbing and surging of ocean tides in order to produce electricity.

Wind power uses the movement of wind to make electricity. Wind turns the propeller-like blades of a turbine around a rotor, which spins a generator, which creates electricity.

Photovoltaic panels absorb raw energy from the sun and use it to create electric energy that is converted into power.

Nuclear energy is based on changing states in the nucleus of an atom (termed "fission" – the splitting of uranium atoms).

All these energy sources have one common trait—rapid change and movement that is converted into power. Human-created power is generated through change and movement. Nature, of course, does the same thing with no human involvement.

With rapidly changing conditions, a still snowfield can become a thundering avalanche.

When earth planes move, powerful earthquakes surge through the earth's crust.

A Category 1 hurricane contains fierce, sustained winds up to 95 miles per hour; a Category 5 hurricane may deliver sustained winds of 157 miles per hour or higher. The speed of the wind determines the power of the hurricane.

Today, it is evident that the power we need to keep the lights on, the freezer icy, and the gasoline pumps operative is generated from sources that consistently exhibit fluidity and change. At the moment of change, energy is released and power is generated.

The more rapid the change, the more power is attributed to the event.

How does this relate to the power of men and women? If life force moves more rapidly through the energy body or subtle physical body that emanates from a woman, this must be reflected in her physical body.

In fact, a woman's physical body is built for rapid, consistent, dramatic change throughout her life. One early proof of constant change is monthly menstruation. The average age for a girl to get her first period in the USA is 12, but the age range is about 8 to 15 years old. Women usually have periods until about ages 45 to 55.[4]

When I was growing up, getting your period was something to hide, to be ashamed of. It was a sign of weakness, something a girl endured that a boy did not have to go through. We called our periods "the curse." But in the paradigm of power, the opposite is true.

Menstruation is evidence of core power. It is a complex process involving numerous glands and hormones, and each monthly cycle has unique stages. I was fascinated to learn about the change and movement that occurs every single day of the menstrual cycle. No wonder a woman radiates power. We should change our name for menstruation to "badass blessing."

---

[4] "Menstruation (Menstrual Cycle, Period)" 2019, https://www.medicinenet.com/menstruation/article.htm

As quoted below from *Women's Health Matters*, a woman's menstrual cycle is said to begin on the first day of her bleeding, if she is not pregnant.

On day one, estrogen and progesterone levels are at their lowest level. The inner lining of the uterus, or endometrium, is discharged as menstrual blood. The unfertilized ovum produced in the last cycle is also discharged.

On days 2 to 12, menstruation continues for three to six days for most women. When menstruation begins, a new ovum begins to mature in the ovaries. The sac around the maturing ovum produces estrogen, increasing the levels in the body. Increasing estrogen levels prompt the uterine lining to thicken beginning around day nine. If a woman becomes pregnant this nutrient-rich lining supports the developing embryo.

During ovulation, estrogen levels peak. Around day 14, the sac containing the mature ovum, splits open releasing it from the ovary. This is called ovulation. The endometrium continues to thicken.

During days 15-22, the empty sac left in the ovary begins to produce both estrogen and progesterone. This sac is called the corpus luteum. The uterine lining continues to thicken thanks to estrogen produced in the ovary. The ovum travels from the ovary down the fallopian tube.

During day 22 through day one of the next cycle, the corpus luteum stops producing estrogen and progesterone. If the egg has not been fertilized, levels of both estrogen and progesterone will begin to drop. Blood vessels in the uterine wall contract and spasm due to the lack of estrogen and progesterone. The uterine lining is shed as menstrual blood beginning the first day of the new cycle[5]

This cycle occurs every single month from tween-age until menopause. How cool is that?

Women and men, instead of sneering, view it as awe inspiring!

This is just one power signal. A woman's body has the capability of pregnancy and giving birth to new life, with myriad changes to the body (pre, during, and post). Volumes have been written on this massive testimony to power.

After bearing a child, another sweeping range of physical change sets in, including lactation, hormonal and glandular changes, and changes to organs and limbs.

A woman experiences higher sexual arousal in more areas of her body than a man.

---

[5] Women's Health Matters, Women's College Hospital, "The Female Body," www.womenshealthmatters.ca

She is capable of multiple orgasms, and studies using MRIs have shown that female orgasms engage more elements of the brain than male orgasms.

She experiences a powerful change with menopause. She has a longer life expectancy.

Think about it. I did. A woman's physical body as a reflection of her high-vibratory energy body represents fluidity and change, which is power.

Of course, in a woman, power is more than physical. It is also mental, emotional, social, sexual, political, intuitive, and spiritual. These factors together are expressions of the innate power of women.

I also pondered how love in men is expressed in their physical bodies.

A man's energy body, with its more closely held, grid-like structure, represents a different quality than power. The energy body is denser. The structure of the energy body resembles a net of interlinked facets.

Life force flows in a constrained but orderly fashion in men. The net captures, holds, and nurtures power in a different form. That form, as the teacher asserted, is love and humility.

When I look at the physical bodies of men, I consistently observe a more solid range of motion. In physical movement, most men project a more constrained gait and posture, and they are comfortable with that. The strength they project comes from this sense of greater solidity. This is beautiful and admirable, but it is not power.

Men experience profound love for their teammates in sports. They rarely speak of it out of fear they will be considered "unmanly." A stable network of energy in their being allows them to interact in ultimately loving and kind ways with known and trusted peers.

Consider Beyoncé dancing – pure fluid movement and power. Then consider Jay-Z singing— a quiet sense of love. Neither person is superior. Their movements and presence reflect their distinct energy beings.

> *"I can't buy you love, I can't show it to you. I can show you affection and I can, you know, I can express love, but I can't put it in your hand. I can't put compassion in your hand. I can't show you that. So the most beautiful things are things that are invisible. That's where the important things lie."*
>
> – Jay-Z

Power is sought by all beings. So is love. The issue is the mix-up. In most cases, both males and females fail to acknowledge or recognize the opposite sex's highest innate traits. In most cases, they are repressing them.

3

THE VISION

Around the time I figured out what power looked like in the natural world and how it was mirrored in the physical and energy bodies of women and men, I began to more closely observe my environment.

I thought most men I knew at work were female-power snuffers, usually out of habit. They seemed networked in their agreement about male superiority. They rarely openly expressed the quality of love.

My women associates were often obsessed with marriage and child-bearing (if they did not have children yet) and measured their worth by their attractiveness to men. They walked, dressed, applied makeup, and groomed their physical appearance in order to snag, hook, catch, grab, or land a man.

So yeah, it was the land of the emperor's new clothes. False assumptions by everyone. Fakery all around. Men made no effort to express universal love. Men were derisive and suspicious of the power of women. Women thought they were less powerful than men and accepted the "dominant" role of men in their lives. Women themselves did not acknowledge or believe in their own power.

I wondered if there was a way to cut through this myopia. I wondered if there was a symbolic shorthand for the power of women and the loving kindness of men.

A few years ago, I traveled in Europe on business and visited a serene spiritual teacher who imparts deep stillness to people who see her (this is called "darshan"). At the trip's conclusion, as I entered my New York apartment, I stood in the foyer and set my suitcase down on the hardwood floor. A question arose in my mind.

"What is the visual symbol for what I have been observing all these years—that men are built for love and humility and women are built for power?"

All of a sudden, I found myself transposed to a very different place.

I stood on a thin sliver of beach. Directly in front of me shimmered a vast wall of water, a huge tsunami wave, fully risen. The wave was so tall I could barely see the top. I felt as if I were staring toward the top of a skyscraper. At its distant height, foam flew off its crest. I heard a deep, megawatt roar emanating from the wave's liquid gray-green depths. All sounds were melded into it—whistling, singing, drumming, laughing, yelling, shrieking—one huge roar. I felt its incredible, pulsing, liquid power.

I knew that this tsunami, risen to its highest peak, was capable of taking any form. It stretched on forever. There was no end to it. I felt it all through my body, an incredible, fluid, pulsing, roaring energy. It was pure, raw power. I knew this massive tsunami was the symbol of women's power—intense beyond measure, fluid, vast, and boundless. H-U-G-E.

Since this was not my imagination at work— I really was standing before a vertical, throbbing skyscraper of multihued (deep blue, luminous turquoise, Mediterranean blue, iceberg blue) water poised to crash down—I barely had time to think "Oh shit, I am about to die." I did think that, but something in my being knew I was looking at a symbol, a response to my inner question. I felt immense awe and overpowering insight, but no fear. I knew I was face to face with my own nature.

Then I had another thought. "If this is what female power looks like, what is the image of male love and humility, the ability for men to be completely at their peak?" As soon as I had that thought, I found myself looking at and immersed in something quite different but equally magnificent—a shimmering latticework of interconnected, luminous, thin golden cables, like a net of interlaced facets in a diamond.

Tightly formed, interlocked joints connected each block of golden cable. The strong golden lattice rested on top of a long, soft white cloud with sunlight bouncing off it, similar to what you see from the window of an airplane. In between the golden grid, gentle cloud wisps floated into the clear, deep blue sky.

The beautiful vista of diamond-like, interconnected golden facets resting on top of the nurturing white cloud – the image stretched on forever. It shone brilliantly, but there was little movement, just the occasional white wisp of cloud drifting beyond the confines of the grid.

In Buddhist thought, there is a state of awareness called the diamond mind.

I knew I was looking at the diamond mind. The latticework of light was exactly as the initial teachings I heard had described it—a male's more compact, grid-like structure, held together like a strong net. It was luminous, exquisite, and boundless.

Then, abruptly, I was back in my apartment foyer, standing next to my black travel suitcase, my tan wool coat draped over the handles.

Ever since that afternoon, this vision has accompanied me. It's in my mind when I look at men and women. When I see men, I sense their energy grid, with grid defined (yourdictionary.com) as:

1. A framework of crisscrossed or parallel bars; a grating or mesh.
2. Something resembling a framework of crisscrossed parallel bars, as in rigidity or organization.
3. A pattern of regularly spaced horizontal and vertical lines forming squares on a map, a chart, an aerial photograph, or an optical device used as a reference for locating points.

In nature, when we see a perfect grid, it is usually there to capture and store something. It may hold together substances, fibers, or solar systems. A bee's perfectly symmetrical honeycomb stores honey. A man's grid-like nature was meant to store something. What better to store than love in its highest, most universal form?

MEN : LOVE

WOMEN : POWER

This has become my new flash card.

I think about the fact that men have a more constrained, grid-like operating system—that is how life force flows through them—and its highest quality, the beautiful and refined diamond mind, is realized through the many rays of loving kindness (metta) and humility.

Women's internal operating system conducts and expresses raw, roaring power, flowing through them to an unimaginable extent in a thundering form. Men express, hold and support loving kindness.

The absorption, clarity, and immersive reality of my vision changed my life. Now all the teachings about men and women and the sex mix-up were no longer theoretical. They were actual, the cosmos knew about it, and I had seen it.

The stunning vision stirred a new wave of heartfelt considerations.

I realized that although the incredible power of women has been deeply repressed throughout most of written history, men's innate power of loving kindness has been deeply repressed as well.

4

POWER SHIFT

"Observe your mental formations, the ideas and tendencies within you that lead you to speak and act as you do. Practice looking deeply to discover the true nature of your mental formations—how you are influenced by your individual consciousness and also by the collective consciousness of your family, ancestors, and society. Unwholesome mental formations cause so much disturbance; wholesome mental formations bring about love, happiness, and liberation." [6]

– Thich Nhat Hanh

---

[6] Thich Nhat Hanh, "Cultivating Compassion," Tricycle, Spring 2015

How could the power of women and the loving kindness of men get so bollixed up?

After the age of one month, everyone wants some form of power. But until recently, only one sex occupied the doorway to exercising power. Males.

Why?

I was a history major in college. I believe that you can learn from history and that both meritorious and heinous actions from long ago have impacted the present time. History provides perspective.

I like understanding the origins of our beliefs.

For example, as I researched the term "agape" for this book, I ran across the name of Aristotle. I had read a few books by Aristotle back in high school but never deeply studied his work. Respect for the great early Western philosopher was like a background program running in my mind.

In case you have not been thinking about Aristotle lately, here is a brief bio from the *Encyclopedia Britannica*:

"**Aristotle,** Greek **Aristoteles,** (born 384 BCE, Stagira, Chalcidice, Greece—died 322, Chalcis, Euboea), ancient Greek philosopher and scientist, one of the greatest intellectual figures of Western history. He was the author of a philosophical and scientific system that became the framework and vehicle for both Christian Scholasticism and medieval Islamic philosophy. Even after the intellectual revolutions of the Renaissance, the Reformation, and the Enlightenment, Aristotelian concepts remained embedded in Western thinking." [7]

I got it. He was a great intellectual and influenced the major religions of the West as well as Western thought in general. Then I googled "Aristotle's views on women," expecting to find interesting insights.

Instead, I found a black hole, a blight on history. And an insight into one source from which destructive and false mental, spiritual, and emotional conditioning arose.

Mr. Aristotle tripped on his robes regarding women. He deeply feared and disliked women. He destroyed women. He misrepresented women in every way. Aristotle was a genuine sexist, and he wrote about it. This is not "he said, she said." His

---

[7] Kenny, J.P. Anthony and Anselm H. Amadio, *Encyclopaedia Britannica,* s.v. "Internet." Encyclopaedia Britannica, Inc., November 13, 2019, https://www.britannica.com/biography/Aristotle

misogyny is riddled throughout his writing, which influenced all of Western civilization through the 16th century, and was basic in the formational beliefs of Christianity, Islam, and Judaism.

According to his words in *Politics*, "As regards the sexes, the male is by nature superior and the female inferior, the male ruler and the female subject." He also wrote that a husband should exert political rule over his wife, controlling her in every way.

He wrote a list of female characteristics. He described women as impulsive, complaining, deceptive, jealous, prone to despondency, less hopeful, more void of self-respect, more false of speech.

Aristotle believed women should not receive any form of education and were just a bit more intelligent than slaves, whom he judged to be like animals with no intelligence whatsoever. He advised that women should be fed lower-quality food than men.

At the same time, he supported the idea that women should be happy.

Are you kidding me?

It sounds crazy today, but his illogic prevailed for over 1,500 years. He was a persuasive and prolific writer. He honed a still-admired philosophical method of intellectual inquiry by posing and answering questions. He faceplanted on the topic of women.

The reason to care about this, whether or not you studied philosophy, is that Aristotle had a deep influence on Western thinking for at least 15 centuries. The residue of Aristotle's miserably mistaken views of women are part of what men and women are still overthrowing today.

In his book, *Aristotle: The Desire to Understand*, Jonathan Lear describes Aristotle's teaching that truth is difficult to reach, but the difficulty does not lie in the world; it lies within us. Lear quotes Aristotle's words: "For as the eyes of bats are to the blaze of day, so is the reason in our soul to the things which are by nature most evident of all."[8]

Aristotle had bat eyes regarding the innate power of women. And for over 20 centuries, women were not allowed to respond. How could they? They had no access whatsoever to reading, writing, social discourse, or education, in large part thanks to the widespread adoption and admiration of Aristotelian teaching.

---

[8] Lear, Jonathan, "Aristotle: The Desire to Understand," 1988, Cambridge University Press

Even today, some religious institutions embrace and practice overt sexism. Sexist religions deprive men of realizing their highest loving qualities because they assign men the role of domination and control over women, a role that does not suit them.

When I write in this book of "embedded" programming of men and women, I refer to suites of assumptions and judgments that were dumped into all of us by the truckload. Aristotle is but one example of how our mental formations about the sexes (ourselves) became twisted and distorted.

Here's that timeless truth again: people try to destroy what they are threatened by. Men, sensing and fearing the vast, fluid power innate in women, tried to shut it down in every way.

Power-draining terms were built into religious and popular writing. A woman "submits" to a man. A man "takes" a woman. A woman "obeys" her husband. The examples are endless. This language subordinates and belittles the natural power species on our planet. The impact of these words twists the core structure of nature.

When powerful women are perceived as weak and subordinate and only men are empowered as leaders, this is a dangerous inversion of the natural order.

A wise teacher, when once asked why women were usually physically smaller than men, paused and answered, "Maybe they were bred to be smaller."

Feeding all women crappier food will certainly do the trick!

Perceptions are changing now. We are identifying and uprooting the falsehoods. But habits change slowly. Christine Lagarde, managing director of the International Monetary Fund, stated in 2019 that employing more women and tackling sexism in the workplace are the keys to making the world economy richer, more equal and less prone to devastating financial collapses.

"I chair meetings at which men and women are present, normally with fewer women than men," she said. "Whenever a woman takes the floor there is a general reduction in the attention of men around the table, and sometimes chatting and gossiping amongst themselves."[9]

We are still at the early stages of understanding and accepting the vast power of women.

---

[9] Elliott, Larry, "More Women in the Workplace Could Boost Economy by 35%," Says Christine Lagarde," The *Guardian*, March 1, 2019.

That power is greater than most men and women realize.

When a man understands the full extent of female power, then he can interact with it, enjoy it, and fully realize his own power – a deep, resonant love and kindness. He can view women through a new lens: he can be supportive as women learn about and express their innate power.

There are numerous helpful ways for men to lean in.

Chris, age 35, works at a Silicon Valley high tech company. He is a computer programmer and manages an all-male team of developers. His boss is a female program manager. When he first got to the company two years ago, he noticed that when she held weekly meetings and presented her plans, his team and the other predominantly male development teams did not listen. When he looked around the room, he saw cold stares, men looking at her slides with a combative vacancy. When she asked for questions, there were none. They would follow her instructions loosely in spite of her, not because of her.

Chris had encountered teachings on the power of women. At the following week's meeting, he raised his hand when she asked for questions. He carefully walked through the diagram of a critical system and told her the analysis was true and well done. When he came to one important component, he commented that there might be another way to design it, drawing from his experience at another company. His tone was purposely friendly and supportive.

The program manager lit up like an LED Christmas display on New York's Fifth Avenue. A discussion with Chris and the whole group ensued. Whenever men tried to bypass the program manager and just talk to Chris, he purposely involved her in the discussion so that every male programmer in the room had to interact directly with her.

Chris continued this strategy for the next eight weeks of meetings, respectfully engaging her ideas in a public setting. By meeting nine, the whole team was participating and the hostile looks were gone. Chris told me he was stunned it had taken that long.

In software development, talented teams are noticed. Chris, the developers, and the program manager all received promotions as they drove their project to a highly successful completion, on time and under budget.

By being open to the wisdom of a smart, authoritative woman and supporting her professionally, Chris did what all men should do — break through their own glacial ice of old habits that resent or just may be unfamiliar with innately powerful women.

When a man understands and accepts a female as an expression of power, he is free to understand himself as an expression of unbounded loving kindness.

5

THE CHALLENGE FOR MEN

The core problem for men is letting go of a wrong, unworkable view of power. We love or fear that word – P-O-W-E-R. For ages, men thought they were the power wielders on the planet. Power over women, over nature, over other human lives. But this is not the case.

Of all the ways men abused power, the most injurious abuse has been asserting power over and repressing women. Suppressing the vast power of women whether by deed or thought caused men to become something they are not.

The symptoms of such abuse are tackled in a blog by Steve Garrett. I like this blog. He starts out writing about physical abuse but then goes on to describe the source of why and how abuse could happen. Any shard of the feelings Garett describes are obstacles for a man seeking to realize his own power.

"From where I'm standing," Garrett says, "it seems that the relatively small number of men who abuse women either don't realize what harm they cause, or have shut down their feelings to the extent that they don't care…

"My guess is that fear is at the root of the male urge to become zombified and to lose any feelings of tenderness or vulnerability – and maybe this is some throwback to the early days of human existence, when everything in nature was a threat, and our instinct was to protect ourselves even in response to women with their ability to reproduce and give birth.

"On top of that, because we were all dependent on a woman for the first years of our lives, it seems that some men cannot forget or forgive the vulnerability and dependence they felt, or their pain and anger when her adored breast was taken from them, and they spend the rest of their lives in terror of ever feeling so dependent or so betrayed again, becoming zombie-men who have no feelings except a buried need to get some kind of revenge.

"Men have traditionally felt shame about displaying any feminine qualities, and have tried to deny and destroy them in themselves, and because females are seen to embody those qualities, and to be closely identified with 'nature', insecure men project their fear onto women, and have a need to 'punish' or control them.

"Perhaps this is why a culture of masculinity evolved that venerates power and disdains vulnerability; and a mind-set that prioritizes finding ways to dominate and control nature, and the women who embody her, rather than living and working in harmony."[10]

For the male readers of this book, it is understood that men and women seek and venerate power. No problem there! The challenge for men is understanding that the emerging wave of powerful women is evolutionary, healing, and a happiness-raiser.

Some men feel displaced by the surge of women occupying powerful roles. Some men have a hard time talking about it.

---

[10] Steve Garrett, "Some Men Behave like Zombies – the Walking Emotionally Dead and Dangerous," The Good Men Project blog, October 2019, https://goodmenproject.com/guy-talk/some-men-behave-like-zombies-the-walking-emotionally-dead-and-dangerous-cmtt/

Author and filmmaker Geraint Anderson wrote in the October 2019 issue of *Marie Claire*, "Many men still have a macho reluctance to tell anyone about their problems… Let's face it, men used to run the show and the loss of that dominance (though, of course, it still has lots further to go) has left many feeling emasculated, anxious and unsure about their role in society."[11]

Anderson cites statistics from CALM, the Campaign Against Living Miserably, a United Kingdom charity designed to support suicidal men. CALM points out that suicide is the biggest single cause of death for men in the UK under the age of 45 and that three-quarters of suicides are committed by men.[12]

This data is corroborated by the American Society for Suicide Prevention. In the United States in 2017, men committed suicide 3.5 times more often than women.[13]

---

[11] Coole, Maria, "Men used to run the show but now many of us feel emasculated and anxious," *Marie Claire UK*, November 2019, https://www.marieclaire.co.uk/life/male-depression-671437

[12] https://www.thecalmzone.net/

[13] https://afsp.org/about-suicide/suicide-statistics/

The mental and emotional challenges men face as society changes are emerging as a hot spot.

There is a different core, illustrious quality that is indigenous to men. When men understand they are wired for the highest forms of love – healing naturally ensues.

6

WHAT'S LOVE GOT TO DO WITH IT?

Give women their raw power. Give men their ancient, natural power to express life's web of profound loving kindness.

Men, please ponder this –

Loving kindness and humility are not the short end of the stick. Life does not work like that. Humans can misconstrue, invert, and distort, but they can't undermine life's essential balance and fullness.

It is said that love is the strongest force in the universe. This is true, and I once experienced it. Because I also had the direct perception of the power of women as a tsunami wave, fully risen; and I perceived the loving kindness of men as a beautiful, elongated golden grid of sturdy, interlocking facets, you may think this is an everyday occurrence for me. It is not. In fact, my experience of the nature of love happened about 30 years ago.

Some people might have had such an experience and changed their entire life, but not me. I simply took it in stride. It is only now, as I write this book, that I am looking deeply into every current of what happened.

The experience took place back in the days when I was closely involved with a national meditation-focused spiritual group. The people and the practice meant everything to me. I went to Northern California to attend a course offered by that group, and I was abruptly turned away. I do not remember why, but it was probably because (though I did not know it then) my involvement with that group was winding down. The people I had grown up with were dropping away.

Being tossed like a piece of used Kleenex out of that meditation gathering hurt me to the core. I was rejected by a group that had been my central interest and family for years. I felt as if I had been stabbed in the back. I got on a bus and wept all the way back to my home several hours down the coast. I was engulfed in blubbering sobs and an endless slobbery nose. My shoulders and chest heaved with weeping. My wound was soul deep. I couldn't get rid of the pain. I returned to the house where I lived in Santa Barbara with a then-boyfriend. He was English and embraced pub-style decor: black leather-ish couches and tufted wallpaper.

I entered the house burdened with sadness. I stared listlessly at the ornate wallpaper.

Then whoa! Wait...wait a minute! In less than a moment, the house changed form. Suddenly, nothing was solid. In an instant, everything—walls, furniture, wallpaper, cabinets, doors, windows – became like a living web, transparent, radiating energy waves that were tangibly made of love. Everything was *made_of_love*. The waves were visual, persistent currents of energy. I had been plunged into an alternate metaphysical reality.

The whole house was pulsating with energy, but the difference from Einstein's equation was that this energy had a clear, palpable feeling. It was unmistakably love–deep, beautiful, and beneficent.

I was not someone who knew a lot about love. I did not have a loving childhood; I was distant from my family members. I had dear friends whom I loved, and I was gaga over pets. I liked, not loved, my current boyfriend. But suddenly, inside the faux-English pub house, I experienced full-on, the world-is-not-solid-and-is-made-of love, non-judgmental, eternal, unending LOVE.

The energetic emanations of love were visceral. They washed over me and through me. I was immersed in a sudden love flood. A pulsating, higher vibration of love. It was unmistakable.

I couldn't believe it. Love was not holding back. Undulations of love permeated everything. It was stunning.

Of course I stopped crying. The force of love was so vast and omnipresent, how could I snivel about a meditation course I was not meant to attend?

I sat down and observed the force of the energies of love permeating every cell of the house with wave after wave of non-solidity. A gentle web or net of love undulated around me. A half-empty cup of black tea that had languished on a coffee table for several days was immersed in love-waves. So was the wooden table.

I did not want the love occupation to end, but over time, the pulsing love-waves gently subsided, then stopped entirely, and the house became solid again. I was shocked that love-waves had made it through that flocked wallpaper. I was humbled and awed.

While most physicists and astrophysicists will not take a stand, I will say from experience that the energy of universal love underlies all creation. Everything is made of waves of love. Not a metaphor. Not a Hallmark card. Pure love. Gandhi was right. Love is the strongest force in the universe.

When I speak of love as something men are innately good at expressing, I speak of this deep, core love. The kind that underlies seemingly solid matter as energy waves of love. Not conditional or clinging love, but a ground state of love that permeates and holds life together.

We believe we sit at our desks and hassle over the details of our bills. We drive our cars with dog hair in the back seat. We eat our fried eggs with crispy toast, but at another level, nothing is solid. We live in a dream we agreed to make real. Underlying the dream is pure love. And, men, you have the energy body to express this. You are built to hold love like a mesh net, a container capable of storing and emanating love.

My friend Larry put it like this. He has a job, a family, and many outside interests. He has been promoted numerous times at his current job because of his skill and his kindness to others. He meditates. He says he experiences a warm feeling in the center of his chest throughout the day, accompanied by waves of love.

"My love for my children almost burns with intensity," he told me. "I feel like I've been liberated from acting like the tough guy I used to aspire to be. I get almost overtaken by deep feelings of love throughout the day, and it's all inside, radiating around me. No one knows. I don't talk about it. I just feel it and act accordingly."

My experience of life as love was not flashy. Here is another truth. Love is not flashy.

Gandhi said, "Love is the strongest force in the universe and also the most humble."

The powerful forces of love and humility are closely linked.

Humility is not weakness; it comes from inner strength and a deep sense of worth and service. Gandhi changed the shape of an entire nation and world with his humility. The athletes we remember are not those who just won the gold medal. We remember and love the athletes who were great but humble. They're the ones we admire, the ones who stand out.

Consider the male symbol – a diamond grid of interlinked golden facets resting upon cloud-like white light. The golden grid is your diamond mind. It serves as a container for higher feelings and emotions. It is still, silent and unending.

The white, billowing clouds in the sky, as we see them from the window of an airplane, do not shout their magnificence. They effortlessly join together, effortlessly break apart, and spread out, with no fanfare. They never call attention to their beauty – they are just over-the-top gorgeous. That's your inner being, men.

Deep love emanates from stillness and silence. The leaders who endure throughout history led with wisdom, courage, and humility. They combined love with humility, not necessarily in words but in practice.

When we speak of love, we are not thinking small. Greatness can be very humble, and usually is.

> *"No one is born hating another person because of the color of his skin, or his background, or his religion. People must learn to hate, and if they can learn to hate, they can be taught to love, for love comes more naturally to the human heart than its opposite."*
>
> – Nelson Mandela

7

VAST (BIG!) LOVE

"Love recognizes no barriers. It jumps hurdles, leaps fences, penetrates walls to arrive at its destination full of hope."

— **Maya Angelou**

Recently I walked into a local bookstore to ask about a book signing event for *Power of the Loving Man*. I spoke to the bookstore manager. He was tall, in his early 30s, nice looking. He asked me for the title of the book and I told him. He visibly twitched with pain. I had to reassure him that "love" in the title was not about romantic love. It was about love of life, of being. His body relaxed. I felt bad he had been so burned in romantic love. I felt particularly bad that the word "love"—the strongest force in the universe—had become a negative for him.

If you say you are nervous about love because it feels sticky and heavy, like oppressive flypaper, then I agree with you. In most cases, as with everything else in our world, we've created a veneer of repressive mediocrity around everything powerful, including powerful love.

Just like my new friend in the local bookstore, you have to push through it.

Does love make you think heavy, syrupy? Fake emojis? Long, cloying ecards with fancy calligraphy, or being buried under two dozen pancakes with powdered sugar and jam slathered on top? Think suffocating? That's not the kind of love or loving kindness I am talking about.

I am talking about the vibrant (not necessarily romantic) love that sets your soul as free as an eagle flying through the air. It is not dependent on one person or moment or condition. It comes from within you, so there are no dependencies. You feel exhilarated when you experience it.

True love brings a lightness of being. It is often accompanied by a sense of lightness – a physical luminosity or brightness in your environment.

A state of love like this makes it simple to express loving kindness. Inner brightness, the light inside you when thoughts become quiet and settle down, is the energy you use to expand and encompass love.

The best thing is, the more you express loving kindness, the more loving kindness grows within you. In financial terms, the more you spend, the richer you become.

Love does not have to be about a person. It might be. It can also be love for a job, a sport, a teacher, a car, a pet, a park, an ocean, a flower, a taco stand, a tree, a home, a laundry soap, life in general…

What do you love? Whatever it is, it counts.

Love is not one thing. It is a multifaceted diamond you inhabit. A diamond ecosystem has multiple facets, all of which influence and support each other. The diamond ecosystem is in balance, but if any part is weak, all the facets can break down. A healthy ecosystem is a self-renewing energy source, an ongoing treasure, an anti-depression and anxiety system. This is how the core male energy system is structured.

Nurturing love is a feeling of harmony, of acceptance. Love (men) and power (women) are designed to coexist harmoniously. Men should never dominate or control. That would be arrogant and imbalanced, as well as a waste of energy. You don't suppress the sea from surging around the globe with magnificent currents far below the clouds. You don't suppress women from expressing their fluid, vast energetic power. You certainly do not get angry or jealous when they express power clearly and directly.

You don't change your very nature (kindness, love) to suppress what you are not: a towering, irrepressible wave-force of power.

> *"I think love has something to do with allowing a person you claim to love to enter a larger arena than the one you create for them."*
>
> — Sting

Consider big-wave surfers. Experienced surfers do not think they will dominate, control, or conquer a big wave. They are awed by the experience of interacting with the power of nature.

> *"When you are big wave surfing, you know the ocean is in charge and it is scary."*
>
> — Andrew Cotton

> *"You stop letting your mind go places that bring a lot of fear association. You let go*

of that and try to be in the moment. I guess the biggest thing is not letting yourself get attached to what could happen."

— Dean Morrison

"What you're really after is an experience of beauty that's just drenching."

— William Finnegan

"Surfing expresses ... a pure yearning for visceral, physical contact with the natural world."

— Matt Warshaw

"Surfing gets your soul, once you feel the wave lift you up and thrust you forward you begin to realize how powerful but beautiful mother nature is and how vast the universe really is, this can't help but put a smile on your face in absolute awe of how beautiful it is to have participated in life."

— Fisher Cannon

The wave is a woman.

Whether you are simply looking at, or are seated side by side, or are intimate with a person who identifies as a woman, try feeling and honoring the huge tsunami wave that is her nature. The experience of beauty may be just drenching.

8

MAN-OBSTACLES

Although men are wired for love and have a deep inner capacity for powerful loving kindness, few men fully express this. What gets in the way? What are the causes of male emotional repression?

To write this book, I interviewed numerous men of all ages, all nationalities. The men I interviewed were open with me, probably because I'm older. Maybe they knew I had written other books. Maybe I am just direct and nonjudgmental.

I only know that men didn't mind telling me about their tormented childhoods, their constant doubt and fear about what it means to be a man, and the negative programming they received about women. Many of the interviews were on the phone. Sometimes I sat at my desk and wept while they spoke.

After about 70 interviews, I stopped. The results were repetitive, and the themes consistent, no matter the age or nationality.

I first asked men about their childhoods and whether they were told or shown to repress their emotions. I asked about their early attitudes toward women. I asked for a timeline – how did showing emotion and feelings change from early childhood to teens, young adulthood to adulthood? What influenced their feelings regarding manliness?

From conducting numerous interviews (and I still do them if you ever want to talk), I arrived at the following conclusion:

Men have been screwed over.

Men have had the same crap mental conditioning as women, but the message was reversed.

Every man I spoke with experienced the snuffing out of feelings and emotions and a complete gut kick in establishing love as a major factor in their lives. Years later, a lot of you guys still struggle with this.

Understanding the sources of repression is liberating. When you know you have a stubborn thorn in your foot, you can do something about it.

If you know you're running on an old operating system, you can change it. If you don't know, if you're using the same old mental and emotional conditioning that was pushed into you since age one month or earlier, then you won't get to experience the delight of being loving and kind.

> *"We cannot solve our problems with the same thinking we used when we created them."*
>
> – Albert Einstein

Men I've met who worked this out took a while to un-repress. They removed one thorn at a time. Now they literally look different. Their skin has a glow (glows are not just for women). The expression around their mouth is softer. Their eyes are brighter and more kindly. They hold less tension in their body – which makes sense since they are not hemorrhaging huge amounts of energy on domination and control.

In a word, they look happier.

As you read through the next pages, see if any of these man-obstacles sound familiar. Every story, every anecdote, is about the blockage and deadening of your internal resonant energy waves of loving kindness.

As you read, try keeping your own notes. Put checkmarks by incidents that are similar to what happened to you.

Here's where the blockages to love have occurred.

1. Wrong Role Models

- My father held in his emotions, except for anger.
- When I tried to hug my stepfather and kiss him good night, he pushed me away and warned me never to do that again.
- My father was never home. My role model was James Bond – suave, smooth, zero emotions, throwaway girlfriends all clamoring for his attention.
- My father was abused by his father, and he abused me at any sign of weakness, which was usually any display of emotion.
- My father was a martial arts teacher. He would wake me up every morning, and I would have to fight, kick, and punch my way to the bathroom. I grew up incredibly angry.

- I grew up in foster care homes. No one was ever overtly mean to me, but no one was ever loving either.

2. Bullying and Name Calling, Peer Group Pressure

- I was the youngest of three brothers. Our oldest brother took it upon himself to teach us to be "real men." This meant drinking, fighting, swaggering, and contests about how many women we could go to bed with. He called me a "sissy" if I ever held back. I dreaded that word. From age 2 to 18, my view of manliness was dictated by my older brother.

- When I was nine, I moved from a little country school with 100 kids to a town elementary school. I got bullied, got into fights. They were emotionally and physically beating me into a different personality. It defined my modern template for social. It was to not be so silly and free. Do not be so excited about life. Spontaneity, joy about life, interest in things – beaten out of me.

I walked away with a more cynical, heavy, solid view of the world. Love of life, gone.

- In junior high, I noticed the girls liked the bad guys, the ones who were violent. I decided to act mean and violent to get girls to like me. I got in trouble, and the results haunted me for years.

- When I was growing up in the projects in New York City, you were one of two things —a man or a pussy. A pussy meant weakness. A man meant no emotions, superior, looking down on women as inferior. Naturally, I wanted to be a "man." Feeling like I was better than women was just part of being a man. I had to fight all the time to be tough. I stopped smiling at age nine.

- My parents gave me a name that could be either a man or a woman's name. My male schoolmates always called me the girl version of the name, accompanied with taunts and violence. They turned me into a girl as if it was the most shameful thing in the world, and they pushed me down. I grew up ashamed of myself, and I went out of my way not to appear like a "girl," a term always used in a sneering manner.

- I grew up in a military family. We moved a lot. I was bisexual and bullied in every school I attended. "Fag," "sissy," "girly" —I didn't care what names they called me, but I never showed emotion. I couldn't be myself and survive.

- I think more guys than realize it are actually really interested in standing up for girls they know in school or meet in social settings, but there is such an intense pressure for them to conform and not stand up for women that they don't. If you are with a group of guys, it's are you a faggot? You don't want to be tagged that way. All guys have deployed that word. If you go there, you're a pussy.

3. Child-Raising Norms

- I loved my mother. But when I was age seven, she cut me off completely because they said a boy should not be that close to his mother. I could not understand it. I hated my father for supporting this idea. It hurt me for the rest of my life.

- When I was at the playground, boys my age were walking along some high beams. I knew my father wanted me to join them, and he even offered to lift me onto the bars. I was afraid to try them. My father viewed me as unmanly from that time forward.

- My father taught his sons how to fish, how to fix tires, how to pitch a tent. He wouldn't teach my sisters, even when they asked, so I assumed they could not do a "man's work."

4. Fear

- I had a deep fear of looking different, feeling different, even doing many different things than the other guys. It started in junior high; I wanted to fit in. I changed the way I looked, the way I talked, who I was friends with, my speech, my interests – everything I could think of to fit in with the guys I thought were the coolest at school. I became much cruder. I bragged about sexual conquests I never had. I turned into a liar and a hypocrite.

- As I was growing up and through the present day, if I show love for anything, I am afraid

I will be taken advantage of by other men. They might not physically gang-rape me, but they would form a circle of scorn that I might never escape from. There's a part of me that still fears showing vulnerability because of this nameless violence that will be unleashed.

5. Hidden Rules

- I grew up without using feelings of love and connectedness to make something happen. I was taught that conquering is my right and ability, the default setting, worldly success as a default. At school, at work, in relationships, my job was to conquer.

- I learned there was a difference between men's activities and women's. It was implicit that there were women's activities to be avoided – yoga, dance class, eating salad, clothes shopping, drinking wine instead of beer. I avoided these activities so no one would call me a fag. I still instinctively veer toward "manly" things.

- Growing up, I learned that girls are weak, easy, untrustworthy, throwaway objects, laughable, manipulative, and exploitable. Sometimes they were smarter than men in school. I thought that until my late teens when a woman kicked my ass in martial arts. Then I started to change my world view.

6. Anger during sex

- I recall in middle school as a guy you start to develop bad feelings of aggression. For girls that age, there's an awakening around their sexuality as a tool to manipulate guys to get ahead or even survive. On the one hand, you have all this lust, desire, and emotion. At the same time, the girls are trying out their behaviors, throwing around sexual energy to see what works and doesn't. It was confusing to me.

- A lot of the anger I felt was that I thought I was the person initiating the sexual attraction, yet a part of me knew it was not me. I felt anger and resentment, but I was indoctrinated in the idea men are better. It couldn't possibly be that a woman was controlling me by arousing my desire.

And yet, during sex, I experienced anger, hate, and resentment. It's strange. I was with this person that I liked; I liked the girls I dated. There could have been deeper feelings, but any positive feelings I had were overtaken by these really intense negative feelings. I remember feeling despondent after having sex with a girlfriend. What were all those feelings that came up? We never talked about it. After sex, I always pretended it was great. My girlfriends liked that. But I would berate myself for essentially having a bad time, even though I was aroused. My mind was angry and in turmoil. I am getting better now that I am in my late twenties.

- When I started dating, I felt anger during sex. I think the anger came from resentment at the control I was consciously or subconsciously aware my girlfriend had over me. When men do not know or acknowledge the inner power of women, when they don't understand that a woman's repressed power which is not allowed to just flow and blossom may be expressed as manipulation and game playing, men get angry.

> They do not understand. It's more of, I know you play all these games, I know you manipulate me, but I don't know what it is you do.
>
> Guys know there is this thing happening, they can't explain it, but they are resentful of that. They've been told they are the dominant ones. Porn taught them that, but life is different.

- As a guy, you are conditioned to believe your experience of a climax is the most intense thing ever. In your mind, you feel dominance over the other person when that moment happens. Science says the opposite. The story told by society is completely reversed. You get angry if a woman has a more intense experience than you do. And of course, she always does.

> Feeling angry while having sex blocked my instincts about love.

Man-obstacles to loving kindness are rooted in our society and consciousness. Unless you were born in the last 16 months, you have probably been exposed to many of these issues.

Everything my interviewees described – all the obstacles you as a man face to diving joyfully into love and humility – are aspects of repressive mental programming. It was pushed into you. It came at you like a missile from before you were born, if your parents knew your gender. It keeps zapping into you through media and unrelenting peer pressure. These ideas are reinforced all the time.

There is still a network, a circle around you telling you a man is a clogged-up, emotionally repressed person, sexually superior and in charge. And it is all 100 percent wrong.

If even thinking about love and humility repels you, consider which of the man-obstacle stories in these pages are still controlling you and diverting your natural, true, ability to be exquisitely loving and kind.

If you can identify the old, repressive, and false programming, you can step back, look at it, and say, "Hey! That's not me! I got stamped and pushed into thinking and behaving a certain way. Now I am going to let it go."

> *"I don't like the phrase 'male toxicity.' It's too accusatory, as if just by being male we are all guilty of some past or future crime. I prefer 'male myopia,' which suggests that society's narrow focus on the myth of manliness*

> *prevents us from seeing the bigger picture of its destructive effects."*
>
> — Kareem Abdul Jabbar

Male friends, be honest with yourself. You were painted with the same rough and deadening coating as all other males.

Just as women were imprinted with feelings of powerlessness, so men got repressed and stamped into feeling superior, becoming less loving than they truly are, unable or unwilling to dig deeper into shining facets of love.

Women are starting to reclaim their power. Now you can reclaim your loving kindness.

9

THE DIAMOND ECOSYSTEM OF LOVE

"Love is a mind that brings peace and happiness to another person. Compassion is a mind that removes the suffering that is present in the other. We all have the seeds of love and compassion in our minds, and we can develop these fine and wonderful sources of energy. We can nurture the unconditional love that does not expect anything in return."

— **Thich Nhat Hanh**

Sometimes if feels like it's been a while—maybe a long, long, time—since you last felt boundless love.

If you learn that you, as a man, exemplify love and you think the emotion is MIA from your life, you have to create it.

Think of the Greek term, *agape*. You might be facing limitations around lovers, sex partners, friends, family, and work colleagues, but you are the owner of agape, universal love. You are the owner of metta, loving kindness.

The range of this search is zero. You are already at the epicenter. You already own many qualities of love. Now you are being asked to lean in. Become those qualities. Dig them up, study them, catch them in action, embellish and store them. Drench yourself in the qualities of love. This is quiet and blissful. Light reflects off you and inside you.

Universal love has many doorways and qualities.

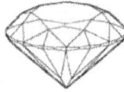

Heart

What are you passionate about? What actions do you perform with heart?

> *"The strongest thing a man can do is cry. To expose your feelings, to be vulnerable in front*

of the world. That's real strength. You know, you feel like you gotta be this guarded person. That's not real. It's fake."

— Jay-Z

"There is nothing braver and more macho than showing love. The boxing community kind of gets it. When someone is fierce in the boxing ring, the old timers say, 'He's all heart. You gotta love this boy.' You kind of have to get your hands dirty. You gotta have perseverance — it's all heart. It really is. I think being heartless and not being able to love is weakness, full on cowardice."

— Jose De La Rosa

"Heart transforms our lives, knowing that we are fighting for what we love. Heart is what gets us to compete authentically with our true nature. When we see real sportsmanship and those competing at a level far beyond their athletic prowess, that is heart. When we see those who graciously lose and do so with every effort, that is also heart. Heart is even failure and the willingness to accept it, grow from it, and

> *try again. Even in defeat, no one can take true heart and love away from you.*
>
> – Eric C. Stevens, Coach – Martial Arts, Sports Psychology, Boxing

Heart isn't rational. It's a term embraced by sports. If showing heart is approved in sports, just turn your head in a slightly different direction and know you can apply heart to anything and see it become vibrant and real.

In the ecosystem of love, heart is at the core. As someone who identifies as a man, perhaps you were told not to display emotion about things and people you hold in your heart. Feelings of tenderness, sadness, sweetness—you know those feelings are there inside you. List them and frequently check the list. Instead of burying the feelings, reactivate them. Look at your heart!

Pick up the smartphone and call or text someone you haven't spoken to in years to let them know you still think of them with kindness and respect. I agree: it is painful to think of the loves we have lost. But why not? They are a part of our heart.

Life is transient. Let some tears come to your eyes. No, you are not a fag, pussy, or sissy if you do this. You are a man. A real person who has emotions and shares them.

If binge-watching is all that comes to mind when creating your list of emotional experiences, then yeah, it's time to get off the mental emotional couch. Find a cause, a craft, a sport, a hobby, a club. Find a new challenge and engage with positive people. Use your heart to feel what is right. Heart is yours already, but you may have to look for it.

> *"Your time is limited, so don't waste it living someone else's life. Don't be trapped by dogma - which is living with the results of other people's thinking. Don't let the noise of others' opinions drown out your own inner voice. And most important, have the courage to follow your heart and intuition."*
>
> — Steve Jobs

> *"It is only with the heart that one can see rightly; what is essential is invisible to the eye."*
>
> — Antoine de Saint-Exupéry

 ## Gratitude

"As we express our gratitude, we must never forget that the highest appreciation is not to utter words, but to live by them."

— John F. Kennedy

"When I started counting my blessings, my whole life turned around."

—Willie Nelson

Sometimes you can't help it. You feel sad, you feel bad. When this happens to me, I make a mental list of what I am grateful for. Gratitude is like a bird that takes you very, very high. Gratitude loosens the hard knots in the energy grid because it is a higher emotion. It is an often-forgotten emotion.

Even when we give thanks in a ritual blessing or in conversation—"Thank you for the lovely kale-and-meatloaf dinner"—we are often saying thanks but not really feeling it.

Feeling sincere gratitude warms and activates your loving being.

Can you thank a flower for being so fricking beautiful? I do. For having a delicate scent? I do that. For displaying vibrant colors? Yup, check. For lasting as long as it can, then dying quietly and gracefully? Yes, I do that. If you can thank a flower, you are on the road to a healthy emotional ecosystem. And you are free of whatever outdated and repressive set of pressure points gripped you and held you in place.

Gratitude is often for unseen things. You can feel self-generated gratitude when stuck in traffic. I do. I self-start feeling grateful for my health, for the pair of sneakers I bought three weeks ago on sale, for my friends who support me in various crises, for the good movie I saw two weeks ago, for having a roof over my head. The anger and powerlessness of a three-hour traffic jam is suddenly offset by the list of things I feel grateful for.

If I can do this in LA traffic, you can do it too. As you mentally touch on each grateful emotion, your feeling comes from the heart, and it helps you let go of the twisting frustration that would otherwise drain and distort your being.

You can feel gratitude when you are in nature or walking along a sidewalk. You can look at a display in a store window and feel gratitude for the care that went into its color and design. You can feel gratitude for the persistence of human beings to try to better their lives.

What you do not want to do is clench your jaw, grip your steering wheel, hunting gun, or suitcase, and close yourself off from your surroundings. When you shut down your sensors that lead to emotions like gratitude, you shut down your greatest power, which flourishes within the diamond ecosystem of love.

Gratitude is mixed and shaken with happiness. Suddenly, from a sense of gratitude, there is just a love of pure life, the diamond is shining softly, and the golden grid is shimmering. And when you say hello to the next person you see on the street, your face is lit with loving kindness. Your eyes sparkle. You can transmit that to someone else because gratitude opened the door to that inner feeling.

Men, gratitude is a door you can open, walk into, and enjoy without fear. And if it ever turns out that your gratitude was ill advised or your trust was misplaced, well, OK. You were still the winner. Now you get to feel thankful you experienced gratitude for a while. Now you can keep it going elsewhere.

Appreciation

"There are only two ways to live your life. One is as though nothing is a miracle. The other is as though everything is a miracle."

—Albert Einstein

Appreciation is another kite-surfing emotional updraft, a state of mind that sweeps away the limited emotional dullness that many of us were raised with.

Stepping back and appreciating something is related to gratitude, but it's different. It's usually based on some mindfulness or meditation (see next chapter) moment where you stop and take a mental snapshot of what is happening around you. The snapshot has more vivid detail and resonance than our usual gulping and sliding through life can capture.

You might suddenly become aware that a friend or coworker looks happy or particularly refreshed. You appreciate life for giving her that moment, and you appreciate the opportunity to see it.

You might have just grilled the best juicy burgers on the barbeque, and there's a moment when you appreciate lifting the fragrant, sizzling rounds from the grill onto a large plate. You wield the dedicated spatula with care. You notice the burger's perfect compatibility with the bun.

You're alone in your apartment with quality headphones on, and your favorite music is playing. Click. Mental snapshot. Music and life are in synch. You appreciate, savor, and cherish the moment.

As you walk down a tree-lined street, the verdant green of the leaves draws your gaze; the leaves rustle in a light wind. Click. Appreciation.

Life handed you those moments. You get to appreciate them.

You, the one who understands your inner nature, can observe these moments and expand them from a small glimmer into a radiant glow. Suddenly, you are feeling loving and kind. You are set up for success in becoming what you already are.

> *"The achievement is appreciation. Your ability to be surprised and awed by beauty!"*
>
> — William Hurt

"If we could see the miracle of a single flower clearly our whole life would change."

— Gautama Buddha

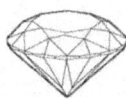

Respect

Another facet of diamond mind love is feeling respect for all kinds of things – interactions, locations, insects, actions, sports, purchases, home décor, tide pools, office papers, blue shirts, teachers, books, detergent pods, goldfish.

We respect skilled doctors. We respect heroes. We respect accomplished musicians and artists. We respect parents who take their kids to the park and play happily.

If you step back from your usual nonstop mental conversation, you can parse back any object and find something worthy. There is so much more to respect.

Where are you as you read this book? At your desk? On an airplane? At your desk, someone took the time to design and manufacture the pen you are using. Someone created that spiral notebook and came up with the spiral design. If you feel respect for these objects, the feeling touches not just your head but your heart. Your mundane world is suddenly a lot shinier.

In your airline seat, someone created the headrest, the tray tables, the overhead lighting. Can you respect these achievements? If you can feel this, your travel will become more magical, like collaboration instead of warfare.

These feelings are primers for love in your being.

Do you respect yourself? Here's a 24/7 affirmation from Jack Canfield that I say to myself when the inner tape of my thoughts turns to self-bashing and accuses me of myriad shortcomings:

"I unconditionally love and respect myself just the way I am."

This affirmation shuts down negative thoughts and restores self-acceptance.

Even when you dislike someone, you can usually summon up respect for some aspect of their being. You may view your boss as a self-centered tyrant, but perhaps you can respect their attention to detail.

When you walk fully into the respect doorway, your grid of emotions positively vibrates with sympathetic feelings.

Respect is like an instrument. You touch one guitar string, and the others vibrate. You are in the land of positive emotions, the base state of loving kindness. And there's no one there to tell you that you cannot dwell in that land.

O Males! Nurturing, helpful feelings are hard-wired into your being. The wires may have gotten rusty from lack of use, true, but a few forays into positive emotions like respect get the shine going. Suddenly, you are lit.

What do you respect about yourself? Do you respect yourself less if you engage in activities that might be seen as gay or female?

An August 5, 2019 article in *PinkNews* described research by Penn State University. The research found that "men may be avoiding environmentally friendly activities because they fear that anyone who catches them recycling or carrying a reusable shopping bag may think they're seeking romantic trysts with other guys."

Several days later, Owen Jones, a reporter for the *Guardian* describing the *PinkNews* article, sarcastically concluded, "So when men are scrabbling around in the sun-scorched dirt for food, or swimming their way through Covent Garden, or sheltering their family from Mad Max-style societal breakdown, they can at least comfort themselves that their precious heterosexuality remains intact."

When you have self-respect, you can recycle, drink merlot, and eat bounteous salads without fear.

Self-respect is the core facet. For most men, it was smashed long ago. Maybe you were short, and "manly" was tall. Maybe your face was round and innocent, but "manly" was rugged and cold. Your interest in sports was minimal–"manly" was the year-round superjock. Maybe you were smart and intellectual; "manly" was the passing grade at school. Maybe you were shy around girls; "manly" was the superstud who got or claimed to get all the girls.

One or many of these premises probably led to a self-administered self-respect grade of C minus. This matters because now, as you reawaken your fully loving self, a lack of self-respect based on old wounds will make it much harder to express and experience full-on love.

It's simple to see.
If you
Respect yourself
Trust yourself
Feel inner stillness
Accept the power of women

Then
You can act from a place of respect for all of life.

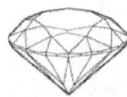

Innocence

"In the beginner's mind there are many possibilities, but in the expert's there are few."

— Shunryu Suzuki

I love innocence. That's why I journey to Disneyland. I become like a child there and find delight in the silliest rides. The singing dolls in "it's a small world" make my heart light up. The ghosts in Haunted Mansion make me laugh. The Pirates of the Caribbean ride always enchants. To enjoy Disneyland, you must agree to become a kid during the time you are there. You can't bring your judgmental adult self to the park!

Innocence is a powerful doorway into love.

At first, it may be hard to return to innocence in everyday life. You are a grown-up now. What does that mean?

Doing new things draws out your innocence. Try a new sport – you are the innocent beginner. Join a rowing club and become an innocent learner. Go to a brand-new place. You are the innocent admirer. Go to the beach and watch a sunset. Tell yourself you are seeing a sunset for the first time. Experience the awe and delight.

Take a walk by yourself in nature. Nature does not care whether or not you will close that deal or win that award. For a little while become as fresh and innocent as your surroundings and feel love for the moments of renewal.

How innocent is a stream of water or a river? Can you find one flowing near you? The water never repeats its pattern. It flows past you and will never return. That is innocence.

Remember when you laughed from the belly, not at someone but because of sheer delight? That's innocence.

Try dusting off innocence. It is bracingly powerful and goes directly to the container you are filling with the diamond brightness of love.

"We've let the blade of our innocence dull over time, and it's only in innocence that you find any kind of magic, any kind of courage."

— Sean Penn

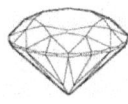

Compassion and Selfless Giving

Here's a wide-open door to loving kindness: compassion and selfless giving—giving without expecting anything in return.

Entire religions are based on compassion. Compassion is the opposite of judgment.

We are all up to our eyeballs in judgments.

Judgment: dumb [fill in the job category]

Judgment: loser

Judgment: lazy person

Judgment: cheap old car

Judgment: bad parents

We judge people and objects constantly, but most of our judgments are just sludge, seaweed on the hulls of our boats.

I study Buddhism. Wisdom and compassion are the core values of Buddhism (besides meditation and mindfulness, of course).

An essential Buddhist practice is called "bodhicitta" (bo-dee-cheeta). In this practice, you visualize breathing in the pain and suffering of others with your inhalation breath and breathing out love and light to others with your exhalation breath. You do this repeatedly. In doing so, you help the other person by surrounding them with kindness and positivity. By releasing your judgments, you help yourself by softening your own hard edges and lifting yourself into a higher state of attention.

Bodhicitta removes the judgment jabber we acquired in early childhood and perpetuate throughout our lives.

When you love and accept, you do not fall into the trap of judgment – a lower state of mind. When you understand that the person you are angry at, condescending toward, seeking to overpower, judging for their "wrongness" has their own full suite of suffering and you consciously seek to remove their suffering, you are practicing compassion or bodhicitta. You are immersed in loving kindness.

The Buddha taught that life is suffering due to desires and aversions. There are no exceptions. A happy homeless person is wealthier inwardly than a depressed wealthy person. Karma is generated by and reflected in your state of mind. Activating compassion for other people is a doorway to loving kindness.

Who have you not been able to forgive?

Who are you angry at right now?

Unpack the grudge box and look at the lineup. Does it include yourself?

As you sit here now, listening to or reading this book, can you find compassion among the facets of the diamond love that are inherent in your male being?

> *"One of my favorite books, 'Natural Born Heroes' by Christopher McDougall, cites one thing as the greatest mark of a leader: Compassion. Not courage. Not strength. Not endurance. But compassion. That's heart right there."*
>
> — Laird Hamilton

Selfless giving is so natural when you love. Some people give selflessly by donating time and/or money to worthy causes. You know it is the right thing to do if you feel a high and clear energy afterwards. Selfless giving means giving—without hope of return on your investment—your time, skills, talents, or insights. A great actor can give selflessly by putting on a great performance that inspires and teaches others. A teacher gives selflessly when creating an excellent curriculum and learning environment for their students. A car mechanic gives selflessly when they go over and beyond in repairing a car. In every case, there is an uplifting exchange for the doer and the recipient.

Selfless giving taps into love and generates love. That's how you know you have found a way of giving that is right for you. Parents give selflessly to their children. Wrapping bandages in a rural hospital may be right for one person but perhaps not right for you. There are countless ways to give selflessly, and finding your ways will ennoble your heart.

10

MEDITATE!

"Teachings can be the catalyst for developing higher states of attention. But they only work when you put your meditation practice to use."

— **Y. Ohta**

In the darkest times, in the midst of suffering, there is a way out of suffering. According to the Buddha, life *is* suffering due to desire and aversion. The way out is meditation and mindfulness.

To navigate the path of life, to develop true power, and to maintain and nurture love, you have to know how to reach inside yourself and experience the deepest, most-still parts of your being.

If you want to understand sex and gender, you must experience your nature that is gender free.

You may have heard about meditation and mindfulness; you may even know how to practice it, but if you want to overcome the repression and abuse of your loving male essence, you should reboot what you know about mindfulness and meditation and consider the following.

Mindfulness

Mindfulness means that you have the ability to re-center yourself throughout the day. You don't allow negative emotions and feelings to take over your mind. Negative feelings include stress, panic, fear, anger, anxiety, jealousy, domination, control, cruelty, manipulation, hatred, and violence.

Normally, when these feelings come into our minds, we are consumed by them. For a time, nothing else exists but these feelings. You may feel helpless to overcome these emotions. Mindfulness means that when negative emotions arise, you use your mind to nip them in the bud.

Consider a thorn-covered weed in a garden. It's far easier to pull it out at its earliest stages of growth than to wait until it grows into an 8-foot, gorilla-size, hand-stabbing foliage from hell.

All negative emotions are caused by mind-states that start small and if left to dwell in our mind and psyche, can become like that humongous monster weed. You can't grow, nurture, or sustain plants in the garden if the bully weeds take over.

With mindfulness, you try to capture and uproot a negative mood or thought at its inception, or even if it has started to take over, to bring your mind back to a clean mental state.

The practice is very simple. For example, you are standing in a long line at a grocery store and some guy you don't know cuts in front of you, vinegar potato chips and a six-pack tucked under his arm, and he disses you. Sure, you want to clobber him with everything you've got, but realistically, you don't want a physical fight. Maybe you were feeling positive and happy before this happened, but suddenly you are in the grip of near-murderous resentment.

At this point, rather than throwing someone to the ground, the mindfulness practice is simple – take a deep breath in through your nose. Let the breath start in your stomach, rise up through your chest, and go up to the center of your forehead. Hold the inhale for a second or two and focus on it. Even while the emotional drama is seething inside you, focus entirely on this strong inhale of your breath. Try to have no other thought. You are just paying attention to your inhalation. Then exhale slowly through the mouth with the same mental focus on the breath. Let your breath journey back from the center of the forehead to the chest to the navel. No thoughts in the mind.

Do this five or six times while focusing solely on your breath, having no thought but focusing on the breath.

That's it. You are taking a mental break, remaining aware but inserting silence into your thought process. This has cut the grip of negative emotions or feelings. Now you are in a clear state to decide what to do. Will it be physical revenge? Probably not. You will probably just decide to stay in line. The a-hole did not get a victory because he did not impress you. He can sense your equanimity.

When you are in touch with your inner stillness, the heavy negative impressions drop away. Heavy, dark emotions are not sustainable in a state of lightness.

If 5 or 6 breaths are not enough, go to 12.

Negative emotions do not leave room for loving kindness. Many men have grown up being told to suck in their negative emotions as a means of dealing with them. Rather than sucking them in and burying them, when you become aware negative emotions are arising, try mindfulness, a practice that has been proven to be effective by numerous studies.

Focus your mind on the breath in. Focus on the breath out.

You are not evading pain—you are just not allowing yourself to be swallowed by it. Your ability to contribute to life and the world is immeasurably increased if you weed out invasive poisonous feelings and emotions and follow your innate path of loving kindness.

Meditation

I have been meditating for over five decades. I love this practice. I am so grateful I was introduced to meditation when I was a teenager. I'm grateful I have had great teachers, read many books, and learned to meditate in different ways.

There is no one right way to meditate. Sincere people may believe there is one right way, but it is simply not true. There are many ways to meditate, and you should learn at least several of them.

The one general practice called meditation is always the same. Meditation means making your mind still, with no thought. No thought in the mind is the beginning state for profound realizations, perceptions, insights, higher experiences of self and selflessness. No thought in the mind is the doorway to higher states of awareness.

Countless studies have proven that meditation is excellent for your physical, emotional, and spiritual health.

Meditation is always done by focusing on something. For example, a sound, a visual meditation tool, a chakra (energy center). We know our minds race around all the time. By focusing intensely on one thing, you sharpen and hone the mind. You focus intently on one thing until only that one thing is in your mind. Then you can let go into stillness.

When we close our eyes, we usually become aware of a torrent of thoughts. Shifting from our usual monkey mind into profound, vibrant stillness requires a strategy. The name of the strategy is meditation. That is why meditation is always about focus. Some meditation teachers say that thoughts are release of stress so it's fine to space out and daydream throughout a meditation. Nope. Sorry! Not true. Thoughts during meditation just mean you have not yet honed the sharpness of your mind.

There are many ways to meditate.

Mantra meditation is a good starting point but not the best way to meditate. As you occasionally repeat the mantra in your mind, the sound will hold the mind at a more surface level. Your meditation period is usually filled with thoughts other than the mantra. It's nice to chant a mantra aloud, however, at the start of meditation.

Guided meditation is when someone speaks aloud with inspirational instructions at the start or perhaps the whole time you are meditating. This can be a helpful way to learn to meditate, but your next step will be to explore the deep, boundless states of awareness inside your mind without external instructions. States of stillness and light are beyond words to describe.

Here is one practice, but you are encouraged to learn others.

1. Sit down in a comfortable chair. Your back should be straight. You can sit cross legged or have your feet on the floor. Close your eyes.
2. Chant aloud a powerful mantra like *AUM* or *SRING*. The syllables are elongated. *AH OH UMMM. SRI-I-I-I-I-I-NG*. Repeat the mantra aloud for seven or more times. Your eyes may be open or closed.

3. Then with eyes open, focus on a visual object. Many traditions use a yantra, a visual meditation tool. You can focus on a single spot on a flower, a candle flame is good too. Focus—try to have no other thoughts in the mind – for several minutes.

4. Now close your eyes again. You have chanted and focused intensely on a physical object for one purpose – to hone the focus of your mind as you sit to meditate, which begins now. Focus on the heart center. It is in the center of your chest. Picture a glowing robin's egg blue orb there. Keep your focus there for up to 15 minutes. By focusing on the heart center, you are opening up the qualities of the heart center – love, harmony, and beauty. When thoughts come into your mind, try to ignore them. Return your focus to the heart center. When you are fully focused on the heart center, you can expand your focus into radiant stillness and remain there.

5. After 15 minutes, slowly open your eyes. Feel gratitude. Don't judge the meditation, and if you happen to remember any thoughts you were having during meditation, don't assume they represent wisdom. They usually do not. It's best to meditate and forget about it.

6. Go about your day.

I vouch for this! When you meditate, your inner strength develops and will inform your whole life. Other people will feel it too. Your inner equilibrium will allow you to see and understand situations in new and useful ways.

Another Way to Meditate—Visualization

Imagine a vast ocean. The ocean is filled with hundreds and thousands of waves. Feel that you are part of that ocean. Imagine that each wave in the ocean is slowly moving through you. Feel that each wave is a wave of joy.

Imagine wave after wave of joy passing through your whole body. As each wave passes through your body, feel that all worries, tensions, anxieties, and problems are being washed away in the successive waves of joy. For several minutes, meditate on wave after wave of joy passing through you. Feel that each new wave of joy increases the amount of joy that you now have, until you feel that you have become all joy. Nothing exists for you except limitless, boundless joy.

Now imagine that you are going beneath the surface of the ocean. The surface of the ocean is filled with many waves, but below the surface, in the depths, all is calm, silent, and serene. Imagine yourself sinking slowly into the depths of the ocean. Here there is only calmness, emptiness, and tranquility. As you visualize yourself going deeper and deeper into the depths of the ocean, feel that a profound peace is entering into you. Feel that the deeper you go into the inner ocean, the more peaceful and calm you become.

Visualize that there is no end to the depths of this ocean. It goes on endlessly. Imagine yourself sinking deeper and deeper into this endless ocean of light, feeling more peace and tranquility filling your entire being until you have become all peace and all tranquility. Continue practicing this visualization until you have ended your meditation session.[14]

Meditation tips

- Try to meditate two times a day, before breakfast and dinner. Sunset is a nice time to meditate.
- Wear loose, comfortable clothing.
- Start with 15-minute meditation sessions, then go up to 20-minute and 30-minute meditation periods.

---

[14] Lenz, Frederick, "Snowboarding to Nirvana," Living Buddha Press, 2018.

- It's easiest to find time at the start of the day. Wake up, shower or splash water on your face, sit to meditate.

- After meditation, take a few minutes to relax before starting your day.

- If you start to feel angry during meditation, stop and open your eyes. Similarly, if you find you are thinking about one person the whole time, stop and open your eyes. You are bringing these emotions and people right into your being. If this is happening, stop for about 30 seconds, open your eyes, then meditate again.

- After a while, create a meditation spot in your home with pretty things to see when you open your eyes. A meditation table with flowers and/or beautiful objects works well.

- Meditation increases your power level and focus. You can complement your practice with other focus activities – challenging work, study, exercise, yoga, martial arts.

- Meditate and forget about it. Do not judge your day by what happened during meditation.

Learn to meditate. It's not "girlish." Meditation is about experiencing inner stillness and luminous, fluid states of mind.

During meditation, you will experience some of the most intensely boundless and powerful mind-states you have ever known.

It takes courage to feel ecstasy and stillness. This is when you are truly gender free. The strongest power and love arise from stillness.

11

SEX

"Blake said that the body was the soul's prison unless the five senses are fully developed and open. He considered the senses the 'windows of the soul.' When sex involves all the senses intensely, it can be like a mystical experience."

— Jim Morrison

"I wish my 15-year-old self had known about my allure to the opposite sex."

— Benedict Cumberbatch

A treasure, a gift, a giving, a loving interaction between consenting adults–that's sexuality.

And if it's not all that, it can still be pretty damn good.

But for the man seeking to develop loving kindness, there are elements of sexuality worth looking at.

Sex can be and often is treated flippantly or poorly, with the results being just what you would expect – a lowering of your love and power levels.

Some facets for your consideration.

Men, if you are having sex with a woman, did you consider you are interacting with a tsunami? Did you notice that her sexuality is intense and complex? Did you give her a chance to fully express it, or were you trying to dominate and assert your power over her – thus draining her energy to the point where it would become the same or less than your own (a precipitous drop for her).

Or did you have the opposite experience?

Ray, 32, was age 29 when his meditation teacher told him about the power of women. He had a girlfriend at the time, and he shared the image of the tsunami wave with her. When they made love that night, Ray told me, it was an unparalleled experience. In her mind, she became the wave. In his mind, he was a brilliant diamond of love. They made love for hours. The next morning, they felt transformed instead of drained. Her inner power level increased. His loving kindness swelled.

It's possible!

Or did you give in to fear about wiping out?

What were you thinking about during sex? Were you present in the moment or thinking about sports or your grocery list?

Were you wrapped up in domination and control, which are negative emotions?

Did you fall into anger and fear – negative emotions?

Did you experience resentment and jealousy – negative emotions?

It's good to know because when you ejaculate, you are pushing your state of mind and emotions into your partner's energy body.

When you have sex with another person, your two energy bodies are thisclose. For example, you are entering a person's body. If it's a woman's body, she is having a much more sensual and arousing experience than you are (lots of science around this). All of her skin is an erotic organ; she is multiorgasmic. Her sexual arousal makes her more emotionally open, and she will pick up your feelings like a sponge.

This is less true of a male partner, depending on how emotionally open he is to you.

Pornography poisons sexuality. Pornography is to your mental health what vaping is to the lungs. Porn clogs and deadens life. A lot of the men I interviewed talked about porn and how it affected them and their sexuality.

When you are trying to experience your loving kindness and running into obstacles, open the porn closet and empty it out.

Here is a brief selection of porn insights from men age 22 to 30.

- My iPad was my gateway to online pornography. I never had a girlfriend in high school. At age 18, I had many sexual encounters. But I was watching pornography every night. It colored my perception of what sexuality is. It took a while, but I finally realized sexuality doesn't have to be weird. I just wanted to have a natural, loving experience.

- I struggled with porn – a multiyear struggle. Porn is male conditioning, a catalog of conquests. I had porn on my computer. It was hard to clear off the computer, and even then, I still had to work hard to get it out of my mind. I had to push back feeling like a predator with every woman I met.

- I started watching porn at age 9 in elementary school and continued to just a couple of years ago. It's like drugs, a dopamine hit. It takes control of your subconscious. I thought porn was a separate container, but it was not. It took years for me to get it. It was a five-to-seven-year journey. In porn, female performers are seen as prey – they are objects to be used and discarded.

- Around 14, when I hit puberty, I started feeling horny. That's around when I first started watching porn. Nowadays, all kids over 13 have porn. You get a template of viewing women in a super sexualized way, like a commodity to have. It goes from a vague wanting to get something from someone, to a strong "I want that." I think it comes into play now for all boys. The early teens are when girls are also pushing it out and starting to draw attention. Porn opens a huge doorway that should not be opened. You get a negative view of women that spans across your whole life.

- Porn is everywhere now. It amplifies my feelings of anger and resentment that come up during sex because porn is about

> negative relationships between men and women.
>
> - Porn varies in how it depicts women and men, but at the very least it represents the lazy way out. When a man is indulging in porn, he isn't putting his energies into interacting with the real world and real women and men in a loving way. When it comes to porn, my greatest regret is the amount of time, energy, and money I've put into it that could have been invested in better relationships with women.

O male readers of this book, pornography and the golden container of love that is your being have nothing at all to do with one another.

You have an energy body. At its highest state is an endless diamond-like grid of refined and loving emotions that honors sexuality. At its lowest state is a twisted, degraded view of sexuality.

If you want to explore your nature, delete the porn from your phone, laptop, etc. Learn what real love is – your nature.

Any porn-induced ideas or superiority/inferiority thoughts you have in your head while having sex with your partner will enter them.

One of my old friends from college decided that she could date any man, have sex, and walk away unscathed. I would see her from time to time and chat over coffee.

Her plan worked well for about two years. She told funny stories about the many men she slept with. Around year three, something happened. She had the same habits, but she looked drained and tired. Her skin and hair looked drab.

She had been ambitious and adventurous. Suddenly, she had no self-confidence or ambition. I asked her who she was dating. She said she had started dating men from different cultures because she felt flattered by their attention and appreciated their wealth.

After talking more, I learned her recent wave of dates consisted of men from cultures that historically repress and belittle women. I told her she was picking up their thought forms and suggested she should take a dating break.

What really happened when my friend had sex with someone who viewed her as weak and throwaway? When a man who considered her an inherently inferior being entered her body, she picked up his thoughts about her. She felt weak and disposable.

My friend remained date free for over a year and emerged stronger and wiser.

Joyful states of mind are experienced during sex. That's how it should be! But there's no joy if someone is projecting dominance. Men I talk to report that they enjoy sex more when they have respect, admiration, and gratitude for their partner, whether it's a short-term encounter or a long-term relationship.

Instead of trying to dominate a woman's (vastly larger) power, you can decide to experience it and let her power take you on a beautiful ride. A man should allow and enable power to be what it is.

In sexuality, isn't it strange that in most cases, across a wide range of gender identities and cultures, people do not know about the huge, innate power in women and the profound love and humility of men?

Isn't it striking that power in women and loving kindness in men have been equally repressed in sexuality during the last few millennia?

For those who've been dating and experiencing unfulfilling sexuality for a long time, it may be good to take a break. When the break is over, why not seek partners who explore agape or metta, because if these qualities are present in their (and your) inner lives, they will expand gloriously to your sex life.

12

POLISHING THE DIAMOND

"The soul is placed in the body like a rough diamond, and must be polished, or the luster of it will never appear."

— **Daniel Defoe**

The first time you went surfing or snowboarding, you stepped on the board and fell off immediately. So you got back on it multiple times until you could stand. Then you added movement, and soon enough, you could stand up on the board easily, stay balanced, and surf a wave or a slope.

Same thing with loving kindness. There are many facets to the diamond mind inside your being. You can start to practice standing up on the diamond surface of love.

Start small at the beginning.

Love Things

- Do you have a car you like or at least appreciate for daily transportation? Try feeling love, appreciation, gratitude for this car. No one has to know.

  You're sitting in the old Ford. You've got the keys in your hand.

  Before you turn on the motor, instead of thinking "is this old piece of doo going to start?" try considering what's good about it. Think of when it was new and shiny. Think of the adventures you and others have had in the car, the places it has taken you. Think about this history it has seen, the roads it has traveled. By now, you should have a slight smile on your face. Feel your heart center in the middle of your chest. Is it glowing a bit, or are you self-conscious about loving something as inanimate as a car? Maybe it won't start; maybe it has driven its last mile. Can you still salute that vehicle and thank it? If not, keep practicing standing up on the diamond board.

- Buy a flower or a bouquet of flowers. Buy flowers that you think look really beautiful.

Put the flowers in a glass or vase and set them somewhere at home on a desk or tabletop where you can sit and look at them. (Yes, it is OK for a man to get flowers and a special vase for himself.)

Try this form of meditation. When you are alone, sit down. Pick out a point on a flower and gaze at it – choose one single point of one bud. It be a color variation or a small texture shift. Your eyes should be open but relaxed. Focus on the point on the flower intensely. Try to have no other thoughts in the mind. Feel love for that flower. Why shouldn't you? It is absolutely beautiful, a perfect expression of its own form of flower-ness. It adds balance and color to your home. It is bursting with its own vast pride of beauty. All the exquisite perfection in the world is inside that flower. It is transient. It will die soon, as all flowers do. But in the meantime, you can love and appreciate the flower.

Even if you are not meditating, just having flowers in the home and loving them is a great practice. No one will know. You are starting to stand up on the diamond board.

What other things can you practice loving?

- Love a treadmill
- Love the bark on a tree
- Love the court where you play basketball
- Love the sheets (or buy new ones you can love!)
- Love the subway art
- Love the pebble on the road where you parked near the dentist's office
- Love when the elevator doors open
- Love turning the pages in this book
- Love your keyboard
- Love your smartphone

Keep practicing random moments of love. Make a list of moments in your life when you stand back and feel love. You are giving yourself the tools to love.

Extend your practice sessions

Since love is a range of higher emotions (high becomes visible when opposed to low – anger, greed, lust, control, domination, cruelty) and love is present in everyday moments, can you set aside a full one hour per day to simply feel love? At home or the office? Hold your private lovefest for elements in your environment. Because love is humble, no one will notice. But they will notice you are so much happier. Your smile will be much wider. Let the pendulum of love swing out to its fullest for a while.

The world is so love impoverished, what's a man to do?

Make Lists

This sounds simple but is actually quite powerful. Write down lists about the facets of love you discover or would like to discover. Focus on the lists, then reread and add to them every day.

- Whom and what do you respect?
- Whom and what do you appreciate?
- Whom and what are you grateful for?
- Who do you feel compassion for?
- Whom and what do you love?
- Whom and what inspires selfless giving?

These lists can be created by category—for example, other people, work, career, and family. Try writing lists of your thoughts in a notebook. A simple yellow legal pad is fine.

After a few rounds of generating a ground state of love, see how you feel. I think you'll feel as if you just threw off 30 pounds of bad conditioning every time you run through these exercises. I think you'll find it is not difficult once you practice a few times.

Have you ever looked at world-class runners and noticed their legs are often longer than most people's legs, making them well suited to win races? That's you in the love arena. You are built for love, and now you are going to put your gifts to work.

Cut the Diamond

Shine some love.

Can you mention love to your male friends? Test out the word "love" with the men you know. Put some energy into it. "I really love Subway sandwiches." "I love my salad spinner." "I love skiing." Whatever you love these days, say it like you mean it, which you should. Be truthful. Take "love" out for a spin.

Can you deal with your friends' ridicule, if it arises? Do you have your reply handy if they call you a pussy, fag, or girl? Well, here it is:

"Thanks, man. I am feeling powerful these days."

Here's a test. You've been going through your lists, practicing feeling loving kindness, and your heart is starting to open. You're feeling a lot happier and freer. You go out with your buddies, and it's easier for you to joke around. Your grin is broader. Your smile radiates genuine warmth.

Your friend: "Hey, what's up? You turning into a girl?"

You: "My power is *up* these days. Thanks for the compliment."

Right. Someone who is in touch with his feelings is truly masculine. Sexual preference has nothing to do with the core values of males and females. Any preference is fine. It's your state of mind that counts. So what your friend is actually asking is, are you turning into an actual man?

Haha. Enjoy the silence at your table.

13

NEGOTIATE THE STREET

"The successful warrior is the average man, with laser-like focus."

– Bruce Lee

Practice love while remaining streetwise. Just because you are feeling like a true man – compassionate, kind, and humble – you can't forget that the world is rough and getting rougher. The goal of a powerful man is not to run around the street with flowers in his hair. If anything, you need to sharpen your external demeanor.

When you're out on the street, be alert. If you haven't learned a martial art yet, go enroll for at least six months. Having a loving heart does not mean you've signed up for victimhood. Have compassion, yes, but if being a kind and loving person in a range of environments is your goal, you have to know how to maneuver around the rough spots. In other words, you're not becoming weak.

There are many environments where you just want to be inaccessible. No need to draw attention to yourself – "Hey, I'm feeling great today!" The people and situations that will benefit from your experience of great loving kindness will emerge. As you become more positive and upbeat, you will want to spend time with people who have similar feelings.

It is necessary to appear tight and strong even when you do not feel that way. Try reading *Art of War* by Sun Tzu. Many CEOs read it. The book is about preparedness, the state of mind of the warrior. You can switch to another mind-state at any time and laugh, weep, marvel, or yearn. A strong, lean self-confidence that others can feel, however, is a great nucleus.

Another trending way to express self-confidence – "Currently not letting anyone fuck with my flow."

Steve, age 42, told me he was working on developing his loving kindness. He liked helping out at a center for homeless people. He regularly taught a mindfulness class there in the evenings. After a class, when he was feeling really high and mellow, he sensed someone following him to his car. He turned around and saw a tall man in a shapeless sweatshirt and a hoodie. The man's face was filled with rage and pain. The man ran toward Steve, as if to knock him down. Steve instantly switched gears from loving kindness to dealing with a potentially life-threatening menace. He assumed a martial arts stance of readiness.

As an aikido black belt (aikido is a form of martial arts that uses circular motions to redirect the opponent rather than injure them), Steve witnessed the predatory energy of his attacker. Within seconds, as the man reached striking distance, Steve used the man's aggressive movements to flip his attacker down to the asphalt as soon as he approached. The moment he was down, Steve mentally prepared for his next movement. The man just lay there, not getting up. Tears trickled down his unshaven face.

Now Steve had to decide. Call the cops or the homeless shelter? He called the homeless shelter. Two of the volunteers came outside and spoke to the man, who was now slowly sitting up while Steve stood by watchfully. They knew his name.

Steve asked the volunteers what he should do. The volunteers said they would handle it, so he got in his car, heart pounding, and drove home.

Steve felt compassion for the man who ran toward him and hoped his aikido response would create total change in the man's life. He told me that after a few days, his own sense of loving kindness expanded as he continually sent this man, who had crossed his path in the most startling way, wishes for change and inner happiness.

Two weeks later, the man attended one of Steve's mindfulness classes at the homeless center. He apologized to Steve and said the precision of Steve's response had helped him remember something admirable about himself.

The martial arts typically emphasize a nobility and restraint that grow along with your physical skills. Physical strength brings health and self-confidence. It is wonderful to feel that your compassion and selflessness are from a center of core strength.

All martial arts teach nonaggression. One of the core tenets is that martial artists do not start fights or bully others. The skills learned in class are to be used for self-defense, only when necessary, and are otherwise shared to build a strong link between the mind and body. The respectful discipline acquired as you go through the levels of martial arts training is a unique experience for most of us.

Many martial arts studios offer training for children because it is often the only environment where discipline and respect will be demanded and built into the training. The experience of going through the levels of training at your own pace is empowering, and it is also an example of selfless giving. Most martial arts instructors teach because of their love of the art, because it made a difference in their lives, because they see how others of any gender or age transform.

Each martial art form teaches its style a bit differently, but once you master the basics, you'll find that you can learn many styles, just as you learn many ways to meditate. If you took martial arts as a kid, revisiting the dojo will be interesting. You may notice a level of heart that you did not see before.

14

RELATIONSHIPS AND ROLE-PLAYING

Relationships

Men whose female partner has accepted them as the control leader may find it scary to acknowledge their partner's innate power as different or more overtly powerful than their own.

I recommend men and women read *Women, Meditation, and Power*, a book (I wrote it) aimed at women that covers the gender-role-mix-up topic and presents the same core teachings as this book from a female point of view. I recommend giving a copy of the book to your partner as well. You are both working on undoing millennia of false and injurious mental conditioning.

In the women-are-slightly-less-powerful-than-men model that is seen today in so many male-female couples, the biggest damage is to the woman who holds herself back to be slightly submissive.

Having a woman in your life who serves to bolster your ego as the "manly" partner – manly in the old sense of the word (i.e., dominant and in charge) – does not serve men either.

For new relationships, you can explain your stance from the start.

She's exploring power; you're exploring love.

Most women will be thrilled to hear that you accept and honor their innate power level.

For existing relationships, I recommend you have open, loving discussions about topics you may not have touched upon before. If you can't have such discussions now, wait. Do your thing. There is no rush. When the time is right, start talking.

What do you talk about? What is the best model for relationships?

The person identifying as female will be nurturing her power level. The person identifying as male will be nurturing boundless love. The man-as-powerful-in-loving-kindness is the best model.

Achieving both sides of your being is the ultimate goal for women and men.

This advice applies to the workplace as well. A recent *Wall Street Journal* study[15] found that women are not only hitting a glass ceiling at the top of companies, they also are not even getting promoted to the first tiers of management. Who is not promoting them? Men in the workplace. C'mon now! Loving kindness at work is a boon for men. Fully realizing their power level at work is a win for women.

Role-Playing

You can role-play with a partner, or if you do not have a partner, do both roles on your own. Smile. Giggle. Dance! See everything from all points of view. The goal is fun and insight (and transformation).

Trying out these roles is a safe way to experience new states of mind. And when you break

---

[15] "JOURNAL REPORTS: LEADERSHIP Where Women Fall Behind at Work: The First Step Into Management," The Wall Street Journal, October 15, 2019.

through the role stereotypes, you'll find the momentum continuing in all your life's settings.

Note that a male or female in this context is anyone who identifies as a male or a female. If you identify as both, then take on both roles. In fact, everyone should try both the male and female roles for all these scenarios.

Have fun and be kind to your partner and yourself!

1. Respect for power

M: A woman is wildly powerful, and I see, appreciate, and nurture that.

F: I respect a loving, kind man who asserts power through compassion and a warm inner happiness.

2. Drop domination and control

M: Domination and control are lower mind-states; I disavow them. In their place are equanimity and humility and gratitude.

F: I will not fake or tolerate submitting to men who exhibit overt or subtle domination and control. I need to express power joyfully.

3. Respect for loving kindness

M: I will not fear getting trashed for being as openly loving, kind, and humble as I want to be.

F: I will embrace and value a man who demonstrates loving kindness as his essential nature.

4. Observe the gender reversals

M: I perceive the power in women and see how often women themselves bury it to please others, particularly men. Many women appear unaware of the vast range of their power.

F: I perceive how women suppress their power to appease men and how men repress their emotions through habit and fear. Most men don't know about their innate loving nature.

5. Be loving and humble during sex (for *eros* partners)

M: It's totally different, but sex is actually much better when I feel love and kindness for my partner. If I am not Mister Dominant, it is a relief.

F: With a kind and loving man, I can trust revealing my real sexual power without frightening my partner – woohoo! It is much more sensual and erotic.

6. Help each other be more mindful

M: When I get angry or controlling, my partner reminds me to take a deep breath. It's like a refresh button for the brain.

F: When I feel belittled at work or around town, my partner reminds me of my innate power level.

7. Watch each other's back

M: I know there are snipers who tear down my self-confidence. We push back on the snipers together by figuring out who they are and what their agenda is. Busted!

F: My partner gets no respect for loving kindness, so I make sure to communicate we are living our best lives.

8. Be giving to each other

M: The secret of a love relationship, whether brief or long term, is for each partner to be equally giving. I do at least one loving-kind thing each day for my partner. And maintain a giving state of mind.

F: There are many ways to be giving. Physical gifts are not the only way to be giving. With a focus on selflessness, we experience Thanksgiving all the time. It inspires me.

9. Laugh at yourself, laugh together

M: We make up jokes and laugh at each other's jokes. All the time.

F: Humor is our salve. We are both badasses. When we get angry, we tell jokes.

10. Examine the effects of your new mantra

M: Women are power; men are love.

F: Men are love; women are power.

15

MORE MEDITATION

As I mentioned earlier, learning different ways to meditate will help you. Now let's enhance and embellish your practice with more techniques.

You have already learned to meditate on the heart center. To go to the next stage, first meditate on your power center, then your heart center, then the intellect center in one 15-to-30-minute practice.

1. Follow the initial instructions from chapter 10. Instead of focusing on the heart center for the entire meditation, for the first five minutes (or first third) of the meditation, focus on the power center. This is just below the belly button. You can find this area by pressing two fingers just below the navel. Picture a glowing

sunflower yellow orb there. Keep your focus there for a time that constitutes one third of your meditation practice.

By focusing on the power center, you are accessing a doorway to the qualities of power, including strength, persistence, and will. When you have thoughts, there is no need for concern. Simply return your focus to the power center. When you are fully focused on the power center with no other thoughts in the mind, you can expand your focus into radiant stillness and remain there.

2. For the next third of the meditation, raise your attention up the spine to focus on the heart center, as described earlier in chapter 10. This is the second part of the meditation. Continue to focus fully on the heart center during this part of the meditation practice.

3. For the third part of the practice, raise your focus to the center of the forehead, the third eye or intellect center. Picture an orb of luminous white light there. By focusing on the intellect center, you are opening up the qualities of deep insight, intuition, wisdom, and knowledge. When you are fully focused on the intellect center with no other thoughts in the

mind, you can expand your focus into radiant stillness and remain there.

4. After 15 to 30 minutes, slowly open your eyes. Feel gratitude. Don't judge the meditation, and if you happen to remember any thoughts you were having during meditation, don't assume they have greater value. They usually do not. It's best to meditate and forget about it.

5. Go about your day. Be kind to others and yourself.

16

IF YOU WANT LOVE...

If you want love, get a dog.

Someone wise said that.

Of course you have to do your share. Walk the pup, feed the sweetie, take your doggie to the vet when needed, snuggle. You will go with your dog to the beach, the park, the forest. If you are at work all day, you will probably want to hire a dog walker in the middle of the day. If you get a puppy, you will have to house-train it and plan on a few months of wonderful chaos and plenty of unpaid labor.

If you do all this, what you get is unconditional love, lots of new dog friends who are as loopy in love as you are, and someone with four legs who always laughs at your jokes.

Yes, your life will be turned upside down until you get used to each other's routines and establish new ones, but the laughter and smiles more than compensate.

Many dogs in shelters are just waiting for you. Something to think about…

17

AVOIDING THE ANGER PATCH

"The best fighter is never angry."

— Lao Tzu

Anger is worth revisiting. We live in a time where anger is becoming normalized. Politicians express it regularly. Social media is deeply infested with it. Some men associate their manness with how much anger they can feel.

Anger is a toxic infection because, no matter how "justified," the person who is most harmed by anger is you, the angry person. As a man, what do you do if a woman is angry, or a close business colleague, or a family member? You can observe them sinking into low states of mind that negatively affect everyone around them. You can practice bodhicitta, described earlier, and wish for their healing.

If we look again at the facets of love, you will find you have the tools to deal with anger, your own or someone else's.

Studies show that both men and women get equally angry. But because men don't feel as comfortable opening up about their emotions, including any angry feelings, they often express their feelings indirectly through aggressive acts.

In Eastern religions, anger is considered a poison. Other poisons are jealousy, competitiveness, hatred, coveting what others have. For men whose emotions have been repressed, anger is a common poison.

Anger can grip you, stomp on your rational reflexes, and throw you under the truck. If you encounter a group of people, all feeling angry for the same reason, I suggest you run, not walk, in a different direction.

If anger is at large in your mind and body, pause for a moment. This is one of the important times to practice mindfulness and bring your mind back to its natural happy state.

You may think you have every reason lined up on your side to be angry, but as one Buddhist teacher said, "When you're RIGHT, you're wrong."

That means that even though your whole personality is self-righteously proclaiming a cause that justifies anger, you are wrong. You are not seeing the big picture.

Letting go of anger is especially important when interfacing with a woman. Remember that her energy body is more fluid and sensitive. It is much more harmed by angry emotions than yours is. If you continually immerse her in anger, it will literally make her sick.

If she chooses to immerse herself in anger for whatever "right" reason, she is deeply sickening herself.

You may want to assert power over others with your anger. What a weak skill. A strong skill is to connect with your anger, recognize it, and let it go with a few breaths. Then you have the freedom to use your own innate energetic ability to show consideration and kindness.

Anger hurts you. It lowers you and drains your energy. A lot of your anger may have arisen through your misunderstanding of the power of women. Now you know – yes, they are powerful – and you know that it is better to embellish your natural higher emotions and let go of the negative ones.

Alarming statistics regarding male suicide were presented earlier in this book. Many experts believe that a major cause of suicide is anger turned inward (against the self). The suicidal person is furious and has no outlet for anger.

Whenever you see a man of any age who looks coarse and angry, he is embroiled in states of mind that do not suit him. If he is angry at only one thing – the innate power of women – that does the job. He is in a lower state of awareness that will hold him down.

Men, loving kindness is your nature. You are a natural at it, just as a woman is a natural at expressing power – fluidity and change. If you are immersed in anger, you are suppressing the strongest aspect of your being.

Attaining a stable state of loving kindness is the opposite of anger. I am highlighting anger because over time, mindfulness and meditation will help you turn it around, and if you find that buried causes are dropping away, then you are on the road to change. You will be able to identify and forgive the sources of your anger. The joy you feel will be your own.

"Look deeply at your anger, as you would look at your own child. Don't reject it or hate it. The point of meditation is not to turn yourself into a battlefield, one side opposing the other. Conscious breathing soothes and calms the anger, and mindfulness penetrates it. Anger is just an energy, and all energies can be transformed. Meditation is the art of using one kind of energy to transform another." [16]

– Thich Nhat Hanh

---

[16] Thich Nhat Hanh, Cultivating Compassion, Tricycle, Spring 2015, https://tricycle.org/magazine/cultivating-compassion/

18

DANCING FOR MEN

Physical Dance

A man I know breaks through his old male patterning by dancing. Not just hopping around the rug a bit but really immersing his mind and body in dedicated dance music. He loves to dance alone so no one can judge him, and he occasionally enjoys dancing with others. I recommend dancing as a doorway to love and learning.

This is his viewpoint:

> "Today I watched this wonderful film produced by Jennifer Siebel Newsom, *The Mask You Live In*.

"After watching the film, I played some music and danced alone in my living room, as I've done many times over the years. I worried my dance was too feminine. But soon enough, I was able to let go. Then I wrote the following poem.

Dance was not easy in the beginning I really cared what they thought of me, everyone I was especially concerned about them judging me less than a man Those curves, those turns, those feelings Not masculine, not how I should be expressing And yet, I wanted to express fearlessly And so I did Little by little

In the beginning, I closed my eyes on the dance floor Sometimes for minutes at a time On a crowded dance floor, I might occasionally bump into and apologize to a fellow dancer, and then go right back into it In this inner world, there was no one looking Only feeling and indescribable movement and energy

Sometimes I let the music guide my mind and body Sometimes I just moved Sometimes I incorporated something from my tai chi class Sometimes I got ideas from my fellow dancers Sometimes I discovered a way in an authentic movement dance class Ideas may begin foreign, but those that stuck with me were only pointers to something I already had deep inside

Male conditioning is based in fear of what other men think of me All those suggestions not to be a pussy, not to be feminine I am feminine I am both and neither Now I naturally express both and neither in my dance And in my dance I feel free."[17]

In ancient societies, communities danced together to express feelings of joy, gratitude, respect, honor, and awe. Dancing together, people shared happy and light-filled states of mind. This happens today. Some people call this ecstatic dancing. In dance, power and love and thought-free mind-states combine forces.

Many men avoid dance because they're not good at it. Perhaps dancing happily is too "girlish." Instead of avoidance, and to overcome timidity, maybe it's time to roll out your dancing shoes.

---

[17] Used with permission by the author.

A Dance of Life Lessons

The first dance

Richard wanted to die. There was no reason to live. He knew he was worthless – as a man, a lover, a wage earner, a companion. He had never considered or thought about suicide, but now the thought was always in his mind. He was a burden, a failure, a loser.

Should he take pills? Or plunge into a deep river where the current would be so strong he could not get out?

And yet, some small part of him wanted to fight back. His girlfriend of three years, Ayla, had left him for another man. He had met Ayla in a salsa dance class. Richard loved to dance. She was pretty and outgoing, and they enjoyed dancing together. When they spent time together away from the dance class, they found they were able to confide in each other. They started dating. Richard was aware Ayla had a former lover who had abused her. She said she had accepted the abuse because she felt she helped him by absorbing his anger.

Ayla often advised Richard he was not an "alpha male." Sometimes when they were at parties or in public settings, she told him when he was not being alpha enough.

Richard's response was to try to become more alpha. One year into their relationship, he was laid off from work. He signed up for unemployment compensation but hid his job status from his girlfriend. Unemployed people are not alpha. After six months, she found out and instead of breaking up with him, she invited him to live in her apartment with her to save rent. The only condition was that they would have an open relationship and date others if they pleased. He accepted her offer.

Richard did not date anyone else. In his mind, Ayla was his girlfriend. She did date other men, including the abusive lover, the police officer she dated before she met Richard. Richard became increasingly jealous. Two years in, the suicidal thoughts started. He still was not working. He felt useless. Every task was an effort. He did not want to leave the apartment. During the day, he watched TV and ate potato chips. He gained weight.

Two and a half years in, the cop became Ayla's full-time boyfriend. Richard wept. The pain of jealousy and injustice was unbearable. Should he live or die? On some days, his choice was death. On other days, he was not sure.

One morning, he woke up and decided to join a gym. He still had some room on a credit card. While he was taking a long shower in the gym, some part of his being, perhaps the part that once meditated and felt happier, told him to fight. He sat in the gym's coffee shop. He searched online for positive statements, and he found hundreds of affirmations, phrases that made him feel good when he read them. "I always fight for myself and my beliefs." "I am good with who I am; I am proud of who I am becoming."

He wrote over 100 affirmations on a notes app on his cell phone. He created attractive colors and images behind the affirmations.

The next day, he went back to the gym and brought his phone. He read the affirmations aloud and repeated them to himself as he ran on the treadmill, cycled, lifted weights, or used an elliptical machine. He repeated them over and over again in his head.

He did this every day. After one month, he got a new job, and he offered to move out of the apartment. Because she viewed him as a friend, Ayla still wanted him to stay, so he did for two more months until he found his own place. Ayla offered to help him move, and they communicated every day. Then they agreed to take a complete break and not speak to each other for 30 days. Within days, Ayla was texting him again, but Richard held to the bargain. She was still seeing the abusive cop, and Richard wanted distance.

After 30 days, he told her it was over. And it was. He vowed never to feel that bad again.

Life lessons

1. Dance is fun, but great dancers still need a reality check.
2. A woman who dates an abusive man will be at a low power level. Her energy body will be weak.
3. Her low power level will drain the energy of people she is close to.
4. Low energy in general leads to lack of self-love and depression, to physical health issues, and loss of opportunities at work, sports, and relationships.
5. There are ways to get out of low mind-states. These ways include meditation, exercise, and purposeful, drastic change. Affirmations can help turn the tide.
6. Most men and women are clueless about their innate, powerful qualities. If they knew about these qualities, they would not make choices that diminish their inner resources in the first place.

7. This is a story of two people making bad choices; but Richard got out alive.

The second dance

It was Sunday night at the Santa Monica mall in Southern California. Someone had set up a huge boombox and was playing a set of disco and hip-hop. It was a free, drop-in dance party. Richard drove by on his bicycle and saw the dancing. He hopped off his bike and joined in. That is how he met Caroline – a tall, unusually beautiful, aspiring LA actress and model.

When they started dancing, they clicked. They met for coffee several times, and Caroline invited him to her apartment. They were officially dating.

Richard dreamed of being a cinematographer. With every paycheck from his new job, he saved for camera equipment. In his spare time, he honed his skills as a multitasker: cameraman, lighting expert, editor, director. He began to pick up short jobs and soon was getting job offers from production companies.

Caroline was often invited to parties, product launches, social events, and show-business awards shows. Richard asked her to bring him, but she would not. She explained she was invited as eye candy, not as a real person but a decoration. She viewed this as a necessary part of launching her acting career, but Richard saw how she loved drawing attention to her physical beauty. It bothered him.

When they were alone together, Richard appreciated Caroline's playfulness and curiosity. But when they went out, even for a couple's dinner, she effectively dropped him at the door and often circulated among tables on her own, drawing admiration from both men and women in the room.

Richard watched her suck up the flattery. He watched her pour sexual energy into the room to draw attention. As months passed, he found himself becoming increasingly upset and jealous. He was not comfortable with her pulling others' mixed bag of energy – ranging from contempt to hostility to admiration to sexual desire – into herself and logging it like notches on a belt. He felt the old, unhappy states of mind he had experienced with Ayla returning. He felt insecure and unworthy, and his self-doubt hurt his work.

After three months of dating, Caroline broke up with him. Richard held on to his anger and pain. Two months after the breakup, returning from a camera shoot in Canada, he landed in LAX and requested an Uber. The app told him the driver was 15 minutes away, so he stood on the curb to wait. He thought about Caroline and felt angry she had dumped him. As he stood there, Lyft and Uber cars veering to the curb to pick up passengers, he suddenly had another feeling. It came on him like a power. In a moment of perfect, pervasive stillness, he recognized the emotional pain he felt as his former path to near suicide.

He had a thought. "I'm not doing that again." He suddenly felt cool and calm, standing on the curb. He felt a power of centeredness enter his being. He was not a needy, insecure being with loving feelings repressed and rejected. That was not his true self.

Instead, he thought to himself, "What is the worst that can happen here?" He thought of Caroline meeting a wealthy, kind, handsome, happy film producer who truly loved her. He thought of her being incredibly happy and in his heart, he blessed her. He even pictured the wedding. He pictured her wedding dress. He hoped she would find her dream man.

Richard felt no doubts. He felt true in his heart. He had dated a beautiful model, a woman whom many of his male friends would be thrilled to speak with, much less date. It did not work. And now he just wished for her the deepest happiness.

When his Uber car pulled up, Richard felt 10,000 pounds lighter. He was happy. His heart was able to breathe again. He felt excited about life.

Life lessons

1. Caroline was drawing into herself a range of negative and often violent energies by playing the role of a vapid, flirtatious model.
2. Caroline probably thought her need for admiring sexual attention was harmless, but she did not realize it was damaging her subtle physical energy body.
3. Richard was picking up those feelings, and they were hurting him.
4. In these circumstances, when nothing could be done, it was time to change.
5. Richard recognized this and emerged from a relationship that started well – beautiful dancing – with a blessing for his former girlfriend.
6. Richard's attachment to Caroline ended when he applied love and forgiveness.

The third dance

Six months after LAX and the transformative Uber wait, Richard attended a friend's wedding. At the reception, everyone was dancing and Richard noticed a young woman with exceptionally limber body movements. She did not seem to have a partner. She just seemed to be enjoying the dance, not trying to attract attention. He wended his way through the wedding guests. He asked the woman, Teresa, if she would dance with him.

They began dancing cautiously, not touching each other, to the wedding band. Teresa saw that Richard could match her dance moves and had some good ones of his own. Richard felt a spiritual and emotional chemistry between them. At the end of the evening, they exchanged business cards. Teresa was a professional gymnast with her own studio. Months passed. Teresa texted Richard with an invitation to attend an LA arts festival. They had fun, and they began dating.

By now, Richard was meditating regularly. He taught Teresa how to meditate, and they began to practice regularly, sometimes meditating on

FaceTime together. They shared spiritual book discoveries. Richard was openly loving and kind to Teresa. He respected her physical power and business acumen as her gymnastics studio grew increasingly successful.

They are a couple today. They live in separate homes. They work hard at their jobs. They see each other regularly but also enjoy frequent time apart. When they can, they go dancing.

Life Lessons

1. Being cognizant of a woman's power at its highest level leads to greater fulfillment and happiness.
2. When the layers are peeled away, men have profound loving kindness in their being.
3. Regular meditation provides balance and insight that is incomparable.
4. Life is a great teacher.

Everyone has their story. These stories are included here because dance is great!

Dance of poetry

> *"When power leads man toward arrogance, poetry reminds him of his limitations. When power narrows the area of man's concern, poetry reminds him of the richness and diversity of existence. When power corrupts, poetry cleanses."*
>
> — John F. Kennedy

19

WE ARE BOTH MALE AND FEMALE

There is no eight-lane gender highway with a double dividing line. Of course all people have both female and male, power and love, inside them. As you meditate more deeply, you experience that there is no gender difference in light and unlimited awareness. We all have the highest qualities of men and women inside us. Men have that tsunami. Women have the shining diamond mind.

But for the most part we see and sense the double dividing line all the time, all around us. People seem to favor (or repress) one side over the other.

Next time you hear or think a woman is a ball-breaker or a bitch, take a closer look. Is she abusing power or using power as she is meant to? If the latter, then *your* mindful mental switch is in order. She is acting out the female side of her nature if she is using power in positive and fluid ways, unafraid of change. Should she also be loving and kind? Yes. If both male and female qualities are well balanced, we would say she is a well-balanced person.

If you hear a man being called a fag or a pussy, take a closer look. Is he pantomiming kind emotions or are his feelings real? If the latter, then *your* mindful mental switch is in order. He is acting out the masculine side of his nature if he is displaying love and kindness in profound and harmonious ways. Should he also be powerful? Yes, definitely. If both his male and female qualities are well balanced, that would be a perfect situation. That would be one happy and respected man.

The male nervous system is wired for love and humility. The female nervous system is engineered for power. With practice, awareness, and the supporting stillness caused by meditation, we develop both sides of our being.

Even if you consider yourself gender fluid or binary, you still have a nervous system and should take a close look at your originating, energetic responses.

For most guys, you've been played. Since you were born, you've been taught that a man stays on his side of the road, the man side. You could show some love, sure, but not too much. You could shed a few tears, but you couldn't weep. You could respect a woman but never let her take charge.

Today many powerful women report that men are afraid of their power level. They tone down their power so they can be with men and not scare the crap out of them. This is lose-lose.

The complexities that arise when people are pretending to be what they are not are staggering. Men and women go through life at half-mast. They walk around looking drained and colorless compared to their vivid possibilities.

The teacher I studied with said the *root cause* of all violence and imbalance on this planet is the repression of the innate power of women and (to a lesser degree) the suppression of the loving kindness of men.

Power is beautiful. Love is beautiful. Men and women have both. No one should be repressing the innate nature of another human being.

When men and women act out their lives based on their new realistic views of their sex and acknowledge the imbalanced views we have had for so long, everyone becomes more powerful. Real truth has an effect. No one is harmed.

It takes time to pull out all the thorns of untruth. Each time another false idea or assumption is removed from your psyche, more happiness ensues.

Happiness is not a selfish state. It's much easier to be selfless, male or female, when your own inner being is acting in accord with its real nature.

A woman should never be afraid to act powerful around a man for fear that it will diminish his male ego. She should be herself – extremely powerful – and optionally partner (partnerless is 100 percent fine) with a person who gets it. Someone who gets it is a person who (if male) is having a wildly good time exploring the diamond mind of loving life and living love in all its manifestations; and who (if female) is exploring and demonstrating all the positive aspects of power.

By adding a strong daily- or twice-daily practice of meditation and practicing mindfulness, gender territory becomes much more open. The rigid boundaries drop, and the infinite boundlessness of any aspect of life, including male/female configurations, emerges. Your sexual preferences may not change, but your assumptions about males and females will. Over time, you are left with a full, sumptuous view of self.

Don't forget that Mother Earth needs you to greatly expand your fluid power and profound love. She has been raped repeatedly by abusive men who blindly express control and domination. Mother Earth needs the human beings who are residents on this planet to wake up and become who they really are. This is the deepest need of our planet – bring women to power to heal Mother Earth.

Loving kindness extends to our environment, to the legacy we hand off to future generations. Should future generations witness an Earth upended by the ongoing repression of the vast leadership power of women and loving kindness in men?

Your inner transformation and realization will have long-lasting effects on the ecological wellbeing of the Earth. Balanced human power can address the Earth's crisis with productivity and insight not seen in thousands of years.

20

THE POWER OF THE LOVING MAN

"Love is an unbending emotion that is a reflection of a higher truth. Love is the ability to extend yourself beyond yourself and become perfect. Love is light. In the inner worlds, it's an energy, a luminescent energy that is the basis of all creation. Love is the only thing in this world that is worthwhile because it is the only thing in this world that is eternal."

— **Frederick Lenz, Ph.D.**

It takes power to make things happen in this world. Power is movement, change, and fluidity. As a man you have that, but in a different form than a woman has. Your male power will be increased by love and humility. Then you are an integrated being, with both male and female qualities.

To become integrated, you do not need to change your physical structure. Your power is developing the strengths you already have.

Boys and men, you have eternity's–life's–permission to be as loving and kind as you would like to be. Don't let the fake men take you down.

Spending the rest of your life working on your boundless strength of loving kindness!

Undoing injurious mental and emotional programming!

Helping others and yourself!

Healing the planet by offering unconditional love and support for the innate power of women!

This is your task and purpose now. This is the power of the loving man.

Appendix

HOW TO GET A DATE

Some men have asked me for advice on dating. Hey, I don't know. But I will give you my two cents.

The traditional reasons women sought out male partners are pretty much gone and dusted. She has her own money, her own career path. She has her own apartment, pets, and friends. She can get her sex toys on Amazon. She is open to the idea of sex with a man or a woman – a whole new gender of competition.

How can you as a man stand out from the pack, and where do you meet a woman you want to spend time with?

I suggest to men who ask me about this that they start with themselves. Remember that women are the power gender, and part of that power is intuition. We are all psychic to some degree, but a woman's fluid energy body is keenly psychic. She can feel your inner feelings.

What is irresistibly attractive? A man who is happy, kind, and loving. A man whose warm smile lights up a room. A man who has laughter inside him. A man who respects a woman's being as representing power and will not try to snuff it out. A man who stops throughout the day to experience the ecosystem of love that is beyond a single partner.

If you meditate regularly, you will become that person. Then, when you go to places where there are predominantly women, you will not be a phony predator the smart, independent women in the room will pick up on immediately.

Going to a class of any kind will give you new knowledge, set the wheels in your mind spinning, and increase your energy level. There are many meetups and community centers that offer classes. Maybe you will meet someone with a sparkling interest in life. Be that kind person with a sparkle in his eye who is fun to be with, and over time, you will get to know your classmates, and there may be one you start to spend time with.

If you have to go to a gym for a few months to remove the belly roll, do it. Health and vitality are not only attractive but great for you. For most people, beer and pot-sticker bellies are not attractive.

Yes, there are dating services, but I think it's better to pursue your interests and share them. You should go through the steps and ideas outlined in this book and make them your own. Implement them.

I can't guarantee you will find a great date, but you will have much more fun and happiness in your life. This is because you will not be reliant on a great date. Your life will feel richer and more expansive. Your kindness and support for the power of women will have helped the women you do spend time with.

Don't pound and hammer dating into a form of your own making, with judgments that may not be true. Let go, be fluid. Let a female partner become a torch of power. She should read this book too.

Become kind, open to the vast power of women, and loving. I think you will be amazed at the results.

LIZ LEWINSON

Liz Lewinson is an award-winning author, speaker, teacher, technologist, strategic planner, and feminist.

She is Vice President and Treasurer of The Frederick P. Lenz Foundation for American Buddhism. She leads the grant category titled "Women in Buddhism."

Liz has authored three books--*American Buddhist Rebel: The Story of Rama - Dr. Frederick Lenz; Women, Meditation, and Power*; and *The Power of the Loving Man* – with additional book and audiobook projects underway.

She began her career as a freelance journalist and soon segued to Hollywood public relations, landing A-list clients in a number of entertainment sectors. Within an eight-year period, she became Senior Vice President of Marketing and Public Relations for Tri-Star Television and Stephen J. Cannell Productions. At Cannell, she managed television series, film, talk shows, and TV specials. Intrigued by the field of computer science, she left public relations in the early 90s and took in-depth training in computer science. She was soon managing complex, multi-million dollar I.T. projects for top Wall Street firms.

In early 2016, she accepted a job in New Zealand as Communications Manager at Utilities Disputes, an ombudsman office for consumers wishing to resolve disputes about electricity, gas, water, and more. In late 2017, she returned to the U.S. to take on more responsibilities at the Lenz Foundation.

Through her company, Skye Pearl, she currently focuses on creating powerful and meaningful global communications through books, audiobooks, film, and other media. To learn more about Liz and her work, visit www.lizlewinson.com.

 www.facebook.com/LizLewinsonAuthor

 www.instagram.com/LizLewinson

 www.twitter.com/LizLewinson

www.ingramcontent.com/pod-product-compliance
Lightning Source LLC
Chambersburg PA
CBHW070426010526
44118CB00014B/1914